CANADA WEIRD STRANGE & TRUE

CANADA WEIRD STRANGE & TRUE

Lisa Wojna

BLUE BIKE BOOKS

© 2015 by Blue Bike Books
First printed in 2015 10 9 8 7 6 5 4 3 2 1
Printed in China

All rights reserved. No part of this work covered by the copyrights hereon may be reproduced or used in any form or by any means—graphic, electronic or mechanical—without the prior written permission of the publisher, except for reviewers, who may quote brief passages. Any request for photocopying, recording, taping or storage on information retrieval systems of any part of this work shall be directed in writing to the publisher.

The Publisher: Blue Bike Books
Website: www.bluebikebooks.com

Library and Archives Canada Cataloguing in Publication

Wojna, Lisa, 1962-, author
    Canada weird, strange and true / Lisa Wojna.

ISBN 978-1-926700-61-8 (pbk.)

   1. Canada--Miscellanea. I. Title.
FC60.W628 2015   971   C2015-902601-6

Project Director: Nicholle Carrière
Project Editor: Wendy Pirk
Cover Image: © bobloblaw / Thinkstock
Illustrators: Roger Garcia, Peter Tyler, Graham Johnson, Patrick Hénaff, Roly Wood and Djordje Todorovic

We acknowledge the financial support of the Government of Canada through the Canada Book Fund (CBF) for our publishing activities.

Produced with the assistance of the Government of Alberta, Alberta Media Fund.

PC: 30

DEDICATION

To Mom, who always taught me to be curious, and Willow, the latest ray of sunshine to join the family fold.

CONTENTS

INTRODUCTION.............................9

**OUR HOME AND NATIVE LAND:
BIZARRE AND OUTLANDISH**
The Place We Call Home........................11

BUILD IT AND THEY WILL COME
UFO Platforms, Full-figure High-rises
and Other Quirky Creations 20
Secret Treasures and Other Mysteries............. 34

**PLACE NAMES, STRANGE SIGNS
AND ROADSIDE ATTRACTIONS**
Putting Our Stamp On It 42
All in a Name 48
You Want Me to do What? 54

THE POWERS THAT BE
A Short Course in Canadian History.............. 56

MARITIME MYSTERIES
Water, Water Everywhere....................... 63

THE COMPLEXITIES OF BEING CANADIAN
Puzzling People and Their Perplexing Stories........ 71
Unique Folks and Their Take on Life.............. 77

THIS JUST IN: UNIQUE NEWS STORIES
You've Got to be Kidding! 89

**CRAZY CRIMES AND
OUTLANDISH OUTLAWS**
You Risked Jail for That? 93

LEGISLATION OVERBOARD
You Mean There's a Law for That? 100
Where There's a Will, There's a Way 109

STRANGE BUT TRUE UNIQUE CANADIAN CONTRIBUTIONS
Canadian Ingenuity at its Finest 111
Cheers to Canadian Culinary Creations 116

SOMETHING FOR EVERYONE
Members Only. 120

WE CANADIANS KNOW HOW TO PARTY
Building on a Great Idea 128

HAUNTED HABITATS
Ghostly Encounters 142
Animating the Inanimate. 160

A WALK ON THE WILD SIDE
Seeing is Believing 166
Beliefs, Behaviours and Ancient Legends 185

ANIMAL ODDITIES
Furs, Fins and Feathers 189
Wildlife Mysteries 202

UNIQUE LAND FORMATIONS
Pingos, Water Spots and Other Anomolies 204

PREVAILING CANADIAN MYSTERIES
Missing but Presumed Dead 219

ACKNOWLEDGEMENTS

An acknowledgement is an expression of gratitude, and no matter how often I've penned the few short sentences that make up this part of any book, the words I've written seem so inadequate to express the thanks I feel to so many people. I'd like to begin by thanking Nicholle Carrière and the team at Blue Bike Books for their kind understanding when life circumstances interrupted my writing, and the final manuscript took longer than expected to complete.

To Faye—friend and mentor. Not sure what I did to earn the blessing of having you become part of my life but thank you. You are very much appreciated.

Thank you to Wendy Pirk, editor extraordinaire. She took my somewhat feeble attempt at organizing the weird, strange, and true facts I collected, unravelled the dishevelled bits, clarified many of the entries and reorganized it all into the book you now hold in your hands. You worked magic, and I thank you.

As you read through this collection you'll no doubt recognize a few bits of trivia, but others will be new—strange developments happen daily in a country as large as ours. However, one can't take a breath these days without someone writing about it on the Internet, in the newspaper or on Facebook. So much of this collection is just that—a collection of tidbits I've unearthed and culled from various sources. Once chosen, these items were cross-referenced with information from official websites. With that in mind, a HUGE thanks goes out to every person who's ever penned a thought, tossed out a tidbit of news or recorded events of significance for official reasons, or just 'cause they came across something too cool not to share. These people planted the seeds that I could run with and elaborate on.

And finally, thank you to my long-suffering family. As I've said many, many times over, without you all this, or anything else I do would be meaningless.

INTRODUCTION

So I looked it up. The definitions of "weird" include reference to the supernatural, or uncanny, bizarre and fantastic or perhaps "relating to fate or the Fates." "Strange" is defined as unusual, extraordinary, odd, queer and the like. Those definitions are like cracking open a candy box full of the outlandish and peculiar and saying, "Have at 'er." Everything is fair game…as long as it's true, of course. And with a country the size of Canada, there's enough weird and strangeness to fill several volumes the size of this one.

Of course that left me with the obvious question: where do I begin writing a book like this? There are obvious topics I can tackle, such as people, places, animals and so on. But somehow that seemed too sterile and planned and, well, potentially boring.

So I started with me.

I'm a Canadian—a patriotic Canadian, I might add. And I've had tons of weird and strange encounters while traversing the more than 7000 kilometres separating St. John's, NL, and Victoria, BC.

My favourite place is Kenora, in northwestern Ontario—a beautiful nugget of lake country that was originally called Rat Portage. You must agree that the name Rat Portage certainly doesn't bring to mind pristine lakes and lush forest. So who named it and why?

Then there's the Treherne, Manitoba, bottle houses and the characters that created them, a woman who designed pictures by biting birch bark, (not in the book) and a strange rock sentinel on the prairies. There were stories of UFOs touching down frighteningly close to our family cabin while other UFOs left strange, circular imprints in a farmer's field just kilometres from our home. My son, who was nine at the time, seriously thought aliens were out to get him.

I've visited a community of yuppie hippies on Vancouver Island, toured a shoe house in Northern BC and I spent the night in an old house on a blip of land in the Pacific with no communication, a creaking water pump, kerosene lamps and no way to get to the mainland after the woman caretaker decided to take off on the only boat available. (The woman was taking care of the house for its owner, who lived in Japan, and she sidelined by offering it up as an under-the-table bed and breakfast. So I guess I deserved that Agatha Christie–worthy experience.)

The more I ponder my experiences, the more I think that maybe the strange and weird is really normal—at the least it's experiences like these and the collection of oddities found in this book that keep life interesting.

OUR HOME AND NATIVE LAND: BIZARRE AND OUTLANDISH

THE PLACE WE CALL HOME

Welcome to Canada, where we don't care who you marry, so long as you both watch hockey.

—Anonymous

The cliché is definitely true—there's no place like home. But if we're honest, most of us have been hit with a case of wanderlust at one time or another in our lives. Let it take hold long enough, and it'll pull us to all kinds of exotic locations. For me, that wanderlust meant wandering away from my home province of Manitoba to the wilds of northern British Columbia and finally backtracking to settle in Alberta—though I'm not jumping at the chance to be called a redneck. My travels aren't exactly exotic, but they certainly gave me a taste for many of the regional flavours this country has to offer, and the opportunity to really embrace what it means to be Canadian. As far as my provincial affiliation goes, I've been told I'm an Albertan now because I've lived here longer than I've lived anywhere else during my adult life. I beg to differ. Manitoba isn't just where I come from. It's my home and the place my heart still yearns for.

If moving from one province to another is challenging for some of us, I simply can't imagine moving away from Canada. And I'll bet for many whose wanderlust pulls them to hang their hats in another country altogether, this motherland remains the home of their heart. In the end, whether you live in a house that looks like a shoe in northern BC, call George Street in St. John's,

Newfoundland, your favourite hangout, like to lounge on one of Manitoba's sandy beaches (under a mosquito net!) or gaze up at the steam clock at the corner of Water Street and Cambie in Vancouver's Gastown, the fancy and flavour of this country is second to none. We certainly have our share of weird, strange and true stories to talk about.

Oh, Canada!

The name "Canada" stems from the word *kanata*, a First Nations word associated with the Mohawk, Oneida and Iroquois tribes that means "village," "settlement" or "town," depending on which translation you use. At least that's the most widely accepted explanation of where our country's good name originated, according to the Government of Canada's Canadian Heritage website.

Explorer Jacques Cartier is credited with stretching the term to include a larger portion of geography, and by 1547 all the land north of the St. Lawrence River was being called "Canada." Our country's name became official in 1791. Whether Cartier's application of the term was a conscious decision or a misunderstanding of what the term meant isn't clear. But it could very well be that an accidental misuse of a word landed our country its name!

Of course there are other theories about how Canada got its name, including one posited by the online Canadian Encyclopedia.com. It suggests the name came from Spaniards who, on return from a gold-hunting expedition around Baie des Chaleurs, located between Québec and New Brunswick, reported there was nothing there, or *aca nada*, which some suggest was expanded into Capa da Nada or "Cape Nothing."

Canada might be a whole lot of sparsely inhabited land even today, but if you've lived in or visited this country you'll know those Spaniards were out to lunch in their interpretation.

DID YOU KNOW?

In 1904, before Alberta and Saskatchewan received their names and geographic delineations, the Canadian powers that be suggested this part of Canada's geography be named the Province of Buffalo. Premier Sir Frederick Haultain suggested the name, but Sir Wilfrid Laurier wasn't too taken with the idea. Instead, Laurier recommended the area be divided into two sections, with the western portion being named Alberta and the eastern portion named Saskatchewan.

National Pride

So it's a little strange that historians can't quite agree how our country got its name, but it's equally strange to learn we were a country for 98 years before we finally had our very own official flag. The predecessor, the Red Ensign, was red with the Union Jack in the upper left corner. This flag also served as the flag of the British Merchant Marine. A shield, representing the provinces of Ontario, Québec, Nova Scotia and New Brunswick was added later, and in 1892 Canada was granted permission to use what was then being referred to as the Canadian Red Ensign at sea. The shield changed as new provinces joined Confederation, and over time the flag was approved for use on buildings that were connected with the federal government, both in this country and abroad.

More than 70 years later, the flag we all know and love was officially raised on Parliament Hill in Ottawa at the stroke of noon on February 15, 1965. As Honourable Maurice

Bourget, Speaker of the Senate, pointed out that fine day, our flag is, "…the symbol of the nation's unity, for it, beyond any doubt, represents all the citizens of Canada without distinction of race, language, belief or opinion."

Parlez-vous Français?
That French is one of this country's official languages is no secret, but did you know that Montréal is the largest French-speaking city in North America? When it comes to size, Paris is the only French-speaking city that rivals Montréal in the entire world.

The Big Picture

Canada is a great country, when it comes to both quality of life and size. As far as size goes Canada is second only to

OUR HOME AND NATIVE LAND: BIZARRE AND OUTLANDISH

Russia, which is almost twice as big as Canada. But in case you didn't catch on to what I'm getting at here, we're bigger than our neighbours to the south! Canada occupies 9,984,670 square kilometres of this continent whereas the U.S. occupies 9,629,091 square kilometres. That's more than 100,000 square kilometres of wiggle room, folks! Oh Canada!

We might be a big country, but we have the fourth lowest population density in the world! According to the World Bank, if you sprinkled Canada's population equally across the country, in 2011 there would have been 3.79 Canadians living per square kilometre.

Bigger is Always Better

The sheer size of this country means we've got a lot to brag about when it comes to weird and wonderful things. For example, even though Russia is bigger, and Alaska sits parallel to the Canadian north, the most northern permanent settlement in the world is located in Canada, in the territory of Nunavut. That settlement is Alert. Alert was named in honour of the HMS Alert, the first ship to reach the northernmost tip of Ellesmere Island in 1875. It may not be a thriving metropolis, but it does boast a permanent weather station, airport, Global Atmosphere Watch laboratory and the Canadian Forces Station Alert. That means people have to be on hand to manage these institutions. However, workers come and go frequently, and Alert is likely the only official community in Canada that, according to recent census reports, had a permanent population of 0!

DID YOU KNOW?

Santa Claus lives at the North Pole. And because the North Pole is geographically and humanly most closely connected to the community of Alert, one could argue that the jolly gift-bearer belongs to Canadians. And letters to Santa go to the Canadian postal code HOH OHO!

Brrrrr...
We Canadians can also brag the coldest temperatures on record in North America. On February 3, 1947, the mercury dipped to −63.9°C. in the community of Snag, Yukon.

OUR HOME AND NATIVE LAND: BIZARRE AND OUTLANDISH

Rain, Rain, Here to Stay?

A region of the Pacific coastline of BC might be called the famed "Sunshine Coast," but the folks down in Ocean Falls would no doubt beg to differ. In fact, they'd outright disagree. The clouds dump about 4390 millimetres of rain on these residents every year, earning them the moniker "Rain People." According to one source, it rains for at least some part of 330 days every year! Singin' in the rain, anyone?

As Far as the Eye Can See

We might have snow and chilly winter weather, but we also have amazing lakes. It's not even bragging (especially to someone like myself who hails from Manitoba, home to three of this country's largest freshwater bodies of water) to say we have some of the best lake country in the world!

But here's something even I didn't know. The longest freshwater beach in the world is located near the town of Wasaga

Beach in Ontario's Simcoe County. It offers the no less than two million summer tourists who visit each year 14 kilometres of sandy beaches on which to sun themselves. Wow!

Old Sow Tidal Pool

There are countless natural wonders located along Canada's Atlantic coastline including the Old Sow, touted as the "largest tidal whirlpool in the Western Hemisphere" and one of only five such whirlpools in the world. With currents measuring six knots, tides swelling to 8 metres and depths charted to 123 metres, the Old Sow commands attention from those travelling in the area. Non-motorized boats could easily be swamped by one of the massive waves.

There are conflicting suggestions surrounding how the whirlpool earned its name. Some etymologists have suggested the sucking sound made by the swirling waters sounds like the noise a pig makes, hence the reference to an "old sow." Others have suggested the name was more likely a mispronunciation of the Old English word "sough" (rhymes with sow!), which refers to a whining or sighing sound.

Pour Me a Cold One
Canadians LOVE their beer, and this country is home to North America's oldest brewery—Molson Canada. Molson Canada was founded in 1786, and in 2005, Molson and Coors breweries merged to become Molson Coors Canada. In doing so, they created the world's fifth largest brewer. Molson Coors Canada continues to roll bottles off the assembly line at the Montréal location where the original Molson Canada brewery first opened its doors. Maybe this isn't so weird, but it's true AND it's definitely good news if you're a beer lover. So go pour yourself a cold one and read on!

Cop Shops?

We've all heard the stereotype that police officers love to frequent doughnut shops for their coffee breaks. But if there is any truth to the suggestion that there are more doughnut shops per capita in Canada than in any other country, the general population's got to be joining our fine Mounties at the drive-through window. Tim Hortons takes the lead with 4304 locations in Canada as of 2015 with a net revenue of $3.2 billion (yes, that is billion with a "b"!)

Cherry cheese Danish with a double double, anyone?

BUILD IT AND THEY WILL COME

UFO PLATFORMS, FULL-FIGURE HIGH-RISES AND OTHER QUIRKY CREATIONS

We shape our buildings, and afterwards our buildings shape us.

–Winston Churchill

In 1972, according to Pulitzer Prize-winning author Alison Lurie, psychologist Albert Mehrabian suggested that as much as 93 percent of communication is nonverbal?

It's a concept that's pretty familiar to us four decades later, but at the time the theory initiated a lot of research on subconscious cues and how they motivate and affect the general population. In particular, the clothes we wear express a lot about our personalities— think Goth versus country chic.

The same is true about the structures we build. American author Alison Lurie wrote a book about this concept called The Language of Houses. *In the book she examines everything from the materials used for particular structures to their architectural style. I can't help but wonder what Lurie would say about St. Paul's UFO launch pad or the Bulkley Valley shoe house.*

Calling Occupants of Interplanetary Craft

Strange saucers flying overhead, awkward creatures with weird heads, flashing lights shooting across the sky. Such stories have been around from time immemorial, and Canada has had no shortage of reports of UFO sightings. But few Canadian communities have gone as far as one Alberta town in addressing the issue of UFOs in their midst.

St. Paul is home to the world's first UFO landing pad. Built in 1967 as one of Canada's Centennial projects, the flying saucer–shaped structure, along with the tourist information booth of the same theme, has certainly boosted the town's profile, even if it hasn't attracted any alien visitors. That said, St. Paul has had its fair share of UFO sightings over the years. They actually manage the sightings with an official information line set up just for the purpose.

Trekky Fans Unite!

A surveyor working for the Canadian Pacific Railway named the Alberta town of Vulcan after the Roman god of fire and forge back in the early 1900s. The town was originally a major western grain shipping point and played a significant role in Canada's agricultural industry. During World War II, the area was also home to an air force training base. Visitors to Vulcan can still see remnants of the original airstrip and skeletons of some of the old hangars. But today, the community of almost 2000 people is more commonly known for its connection to a Hollywood sci-fi favourite.

That connection began when the entrepreneurial people of Vulcan saw a clever way to connect their small prairie community to the popularity of the television series *Star Trek*. The show first aired in 1966, long after the town of Vulcan got its name. And although the *Star Trek* series as a whole has undergone several changes since then, it's maintained a wide fan base. For the residents of Vulcan to tie their town's name to the fictional planet of the same name, home to Mr. Spock, one of the show's main characters, was a wonderful—and profitable—bit of whimsy.

Over the years the town has continued to build on its Trekky connection, beginning with the creation of the Tourism and Trek Station. The building not only provides visitors with information on the town of Vulcan, it also includes its own collection of *Star Trek* memorabilia, along with a chance to participate in a virtual reality game *The Vulcan Space Adventure*. A replica of the show's USS *Enterprise*, the TrekCetera Star Trek museum and space-themed murals dotting the town's buildings are part of the overall Vulcan experience. You can also enjoy its popular "Spock Days" convention, now called Vul-Con, a festival where participants dress up like Star Trek characters and participate in a number of theme-related activities.

Since the first annual Spock Days convention in 1993, a steady stream of *Star Trek* elite has visited this Alberta wonder. Even Leonard Nimoy, the American actor best known for his role as Spock, took in Spock Days during a visit to Alberta in 2010.

Marble Memorials

The Taj Mahal is a magnificent palace erected as an expression of love in the midst of grief. Mughal emperor Shah Jahan commissioned the building, located in Agra, Uttar Pradesh, India, after his third (and favourite) wife, Mumtaz Mahal, died. If photos of the building are any indication, a visit to the site would be unforgettable.

The UNESCO World Heritage Site was so inspirational to one Canadian, that following his visit to the palace, Toronto resident Thomas Foster decided to build his own version of the Taj Mahal to serve as a final resting place for himself, his wife and his daughter.

It cost $250,000 and took almost two years to build, but the end result, completed in 1936, captured all the majesty of its Indian inspiration.

According to the official website, the building was constructed of "Indiana limestone on an octagonal base, culminating in a great central dome sheathed in copper." Large archways, marble columns, bronze door and window finishings, stained glass windows and Christian symbols etched into marble mosaics are just some of the characteristics that make this attraction, located in Foster's hometown of Ontario Township of Uxbridge, a major tourist draw.

Today, the Township of Uxbridge owns and maintains the building. In 1996 it received historic designation. Foster was interred in his architectural masterpiece in 1945 at the age of 93.

Crowded Quarters?

According to a 2013 CBC report, with every passing year Canadian prisons become "more crowded, more violent and almost devoid of any sense of rehabilitation." It's a good thing, then, that Ontario's Rodney Jailhouse, built in 1890, is now abandoned. When is was operational, the jailhouse measured a scant 4.5 x 5.4 metres (or 24.3 metres squared), making it not just the smallest jail in Canada, but one of the smallest in North America. Today it still stands as a testament to another time, but it now operates as a tourist information centre.

Quick Exit

Another Canadian community claiming one of the country's smallest jails is Coboconk, Ontario. The Coboconk (or Coby) jail measured 4.57 x 8.84 metres, which is slightly larger than the jail in Rodney. However, the Coby jail is probably the only one of its kind that had an escape route built in.

The story goes that Albert Ryckman, the gent responsible for erecting the structure, allegedly left the mortar off several bricks. That way, should he ever find himself in the unfortunate position of being incarcerated after a night of revelry, he'd have an easy escape route. Legend has it that Ryckman made good use of his secret exit!

BUILD IT AND THEY WILL COME

Man-made Forest

A homesick American working on the Alaska Highway began this uniquely Canadian construct back in 1942. Private Carl K. Lindley from Company D, 341st Army of Engineers, found himself recuperating from a workplace injury in what was then a military air base. Though convalescing, he was still mobile—and likely bored—so his commanding officer got him to do some maintenance work that included repainting the directional post. Longing for home, Lindley added a new sign to the post—Danville, Illinois, and the distance from what today is the town of Watson Lake. It got other soldiers wanting to do the same, and pretty soon visitors to the area joined in by adding signs of their own.

The tradition has continued to this day, with more than 100,000 place signs making up the only "forest" of its kind in the world, the "Sign Post Forest."

A Man's Home is His Castle

This is one story I can personally attest to. I've seen it myself. Got the pictures. Wrote the story for the *Smithers Interior News* back in the 1990s. But it's an oddity that bears repeating in a collection dedicated to Canadian oddities. Turn off Highway 16 on Kitseguecla Lake Road, which is near the midway point between the town of Smithers and Moricetown in British Columbia's scenic Bulkley Valley. Motor along for about 10 kilometres, and you'll find a shoe. Not just any old shoe, mind you. You'll come across a shoe worthy of the little old woman of nursery rhyme fame. Built in the 1980s, the house began as a trailer and was built up from there. It's small but homey and serves as quite the surprise to unsuspecting motorists out for a scenic drive.

Cold Comfort

Speaking of castles, imagine building one, along with all its furniture, cupboards and so on, only to have it melt three months later, leaving you no choice but to build it again. Stranger still, imagine paying, and paying quite dearly, for the privilege of staying at this vanishing establishment, constructed of 400 tonnes of ice and 12,000 tonnes of snow! Although this weird Canadian experience isn't the first of its kind in the world, it's certainly a first in North America.

Since 2001, the ice structure known as Hôtel de Glace, 10 minutes from beautiful downtown Québec City, has hosted visitors looking for a unique, albeit chilly, winter vacation experience. Everything—even the base for the bed you'll sleep in—is constructed of ice. And it's really not that cold, or so the company's fact sheet claims.

CEO Jacques Desbois was the mover behind this business venture. One can't help but think that when he first proposed the idea of building a hotel from ice, potential investors must have scoffed at the idea. But Desbois had a prototype to build from. The folks over in Jukkasjarvi, Sweden, have been successfully hosting visitors since they opened their first—and the world's first—ice hotel in 1990. If the Swedes can do it, why can't the Québecois?

Desbois sold his idea to Yvon Guerard and Michel Mordret, who initially signed on for the venture. For more than a decade honeymooners, families and outdoor enthusiasts have flocked to Hôtel de Glace for a remarkable experience. With that kind of track record, naysayers who initially thought Desbois was a few screws short of a toolbox have had to eat crow.

Successful or not, you still have to agree that vacationing on a slab of ice is a tad odd. The hotel's website promises a romantic getaway but also suggests you pack clothing made of wool, flannel or polar fleece, as well as long underwear. The hotel provides visitors with arctic sleeping bags that promise to keep you warm even if the temperatures dip to −30°C. (So much for kindling a fire of your own making.) Of course temperatures inside the hotel never dip down that low. Climate conditions inside the hotel are described as "ambient"; the ice acts as an insulator so even if outside temperatures drop significantly, the interior of the hotel remains between −3 and −5°C. If photographs of the hotel are any indication it looks like Nordic sweaters and down-filled jackets are typical indoor wear.

There are countless pictures of the Hôtel de Glace on the Internet, and I must admit they all look intriguing, maybe even inviting. But I still can't shake the thought that should I ever visit there, I'd be dreaming about hot showers until I returned home.

DID YOU KNOW?

Two kilometres underground, in what once was the Vale Creighton Mine, is Canada's only underground science laboratory. The Sudbury Neutrino Observatory laboratory (SNOLAB) is located near Sudbury and was started as a joint project by the universities of British Columbia, Guelph and Montréal, as well as Carleton, Laurentian and Queen's universities. The idea was to use the facility to conduct underground physics experiments that required extreme levels of cleanliness—something this lab can provide. According to its website, SNOLAB's main focus was low energy solar neutrinos, neutrinoless double beta decay, cosmic dark matter searches, and supernova neutrino searches. More recently, the lab has expanded its interests to include the fields of seismology and geophysics, as well as underground life. If you want detailed information on what exactly these topics entail, you'll need to speak with a scientist. However, I can tell you that they basically involve a study of astroparticle physics, which is the study of subatomic particles that are associated with astronomical sources.

Clear as mud? I agree.

Absolutely Amazing!

This twin tower residential condominium, part of a five-tower city centre development, boasts curves worthy of Marilyn Monroe fame; hence its nickname "Marilyn Monroe Towers." Otherwise known as Absolute World, these two skyscrapers tower over the surrounding city of Mississauga, Ontario, rising 50 and 56 floors respectively. What makes them so unique is that the buildings were engineered to twist from their base at specific degrees at each floor, giving the buildings a curvy, almost hourglass shape, just like their namesake.

Guiding Light?

Hold on to your hats, everyone—Saskatchewan can actually boast its own working lighthouse!

Yup, there is more to Saskatchewan than flat prairie!

The idea of building a lighthouse in the resort village of Cochin, located about 35 kilometres north of North Battleford, was the brainchild of its first mayor, Tom Archdekin. He suggested the lighthouse in 1988 as a tourism project, and by the following spring all stakeholders, including the village council, had given their approval. The land chosen for the proposed lighthouse was a hill located at the north end of the village, overlooking Murray and Jackfish Lakes. The land was privately owned by the Pirot family, and they were more than thrilled with the idea. There is a 158-step climb up the hill to the 11.5 metre high lighthouse, giving visitors a panoramic view that could rival any other scenic wonder this country has to offer. And because it's a working lighthouse, it offers summer boaters and winter Ski-doo enthusiasts a guiding light in poor weather conditions.

Weird and practical!

Cross Country Connection

Outlook, a town in west-central Saskatchewan, is typical of many small prairie communities. Early settlers in the area tamed the land and set up farms. If they were lucky, nearby communities erupted when the Canadian Pacific Railway (CPR) decided the location suited their ever expanding endeavours.

In the case of Outlook, the CPR began auctioning lots in August 1908, which officially established the village. By November of the same year, train service between the growing community and Moose Jaw was running three times a week. Before long, CPR officials felt the need to build a bridge across the South Saskatchewan River. It was a 1.2 kilometre long feat that, by its completion, would cost the company $1 million—a staggering amount for its time. Work began on the project in 1910 and finished in 1912.

At the time of the bridge's construction, the nine concrete piers rising from the river to support the bridge structure measured 45 metres, making them the highest concrete piers in the world. Original plans included an attached traffic bridge and footbridge, but when it was decided the structure wasn't adequate for those additions, the traffic bridge was scrapped and the footbridge dismantled.

The first train crossed the Skytrail Bridge on October 23, 1912. For 75 years the bridge sustained regular rail traffic until it was decommissioned on March 16, 1987.

OLD STRUCTURE, NEW IDEA
The trains may have stopped but the structure remained, a prairie sentinel watching over the community it so faithfully served. It seemed a waste to simply abandon it to the elements, and the clever folks in Outlook thought of another way to use their amazing structure. Why not somehow connect Outlook to the Trans Canada Trail system, which conveniently wound through their community from Moose Jaw on its way to Saskatoon? When it is complete, the trail, the construction of which began in 1992 as a national project celebrating the country's 125th birthday, will cover almost 24,000 kilometres from ocean to ocean and into the territories, making it "one of the world's largest networks of multi-use recreational trails."

In 2003, the idea of converting the bridge and using it as part of the cross-country trail system blossomed to a potential reality when the town received a grant of free labour from the 2003 Bridges for Canada program, established as part of the Centennial of Military Engineers (CME). The town of Outlook and the rural municipality of Rudy advanced the money needed for materials until organizers were able to raise the required funds.

The Skytrail Bridge now stands as an integral part of the Trans Canada Trail system, but that's only part of its claim to fame. When it was completed in 2004, the Skytrail became one of the longest pedestrian bridges in the country.

DID YOU KNOW?

As of the writing of this book, more than 17,000 kilometres, roughly 75 percent of the Trans Canada Trail is complete. The almost 500 trails that make up the route thus far connect more than 1000 communities. Organizers state that four of every five Canadians live within 30 minutes of the trail.

Glass Village

Get an idea in our heads, and there's no telling where that can lead us. Most often, we're probably in for more than we bargained for. When Bob and Dora Cain of Treherne, Manitoba, decided it would be fun to build a house out of bottles, they had no idea how many bottles they'd need; Dora scrubbed labels off 4000 before her husband and a family friend, Fred Harp, began construction. It took the men two months of constant work before the first house, on the Cain's farm, was completed in 1979. Mother Cain was in desperate need of a manicure by that point.

Meanwhile, the trio got to thinking—one glass house was cool, but a second structure would make it doubly cool. So in 1983, they were at it again. This time their goal was to build a church. This time Dora needed to scrub 5000 bottles, significantly increasing the cost of any manicure.

This time it took almost three months to build; churches require considerably more accoutrements than a house would. When it was finished, their church boasted one stained glass window donated by Cypress River's Anglican

Church and a second from a private home in Winnipeg. Bob scavenged for pews, sawed them in two and provided seating for visitors, which was a good thing because the church played host to at least three weddings.

When I visited the Treherne glass buildings in the early 1990s, the Cains had already added a wishing well and a useable bathroom—all constructed of bottles, although a few pieces of wood were added to the privy for privacy reasons. The church was majestic with natural light flooding into the building and creating a kind of ethereal feeling. And the Cains—well, they were as lovely and hospitable as one would expect the kind of people who live in, or build, glass houses would be.

More than 7000 visitors visited the Cains' rural property during most summers between 1979 and 2007, when the buildings were moved and incorporated into a park in the town of Treherne.

SECRET TREASURES AND OTHER MYSTERIES

Ancient Echoes

Now I've got to admit that I've walked through Manitoba's Legislative Buildings, marvelled at the architecture, and wondered about the archaic décor. But it was news to me that a researcher spent a decade of his life researching the symbols within these buildings, and has since led tours explaining what they all mean and who was responsible for their installation. Dr. Frank Albo, an "architectural historian and an expert on communicating new streams of knowledge in relation to the built environment and the cultures of the past," penned a bestselling book called *The Hermetic Code*, which revealed the secrets of the Manitoba Legislature. In particular, Albo suggests Freemasonry philosophy was intimately involved in the architectural choices because, he posits, many of the builders were likely Freemasons.

Bison and lion head sculptures aside, perhaps the biggest contribution these longstanding buildings have made to the collection of Manitoba mysteries is the Pool of the Black Star. In December 2013, more than four dozen people gathered around the Black Star, sitting in meditative poses and hoping for some insight into the deeper mysteries posed by that particular symbol. I'm not sure if they learned anything more than Albo's insight into the topic, but many reported the experience offered them a chance to experience deeper "cleansing," "peace" and "more experience."

Historic Graffiti

More often than not, human alterations to Mother Nature's masterpieces are discouraged. But in the case of Roche Percee, Saskatchewan, First Nations' carvings, coupled with the autographs of early explorers, U.S. Cavalrymen, members of the North-West Mounted Police (NWMP) and surveyors who moved through the area are a human touch that add to the historic significance of the site.

Another large assortment of petroglyphs can also be found in Cypress Hills. But perhaps one of Saskatchewan's most mysterious collections of unique rocks can be found on the horizontal surface of a flat sandstone cliff in St. Victor Petroglyphs Provincial Park, located in the south central area of the province. Here, more than 300 assorted carvings, including animal tracks, human handprints and footprints, faces, depictions of the plains grizzly bear and other images have been discovered.

Although archaeologists date these petroglyphs to sometime between 500 and 1700 CE, there is no definitive theory on who created them or why. Because of natural erosion, the images have become quite shallow. Park officials suggest the best time to see them is on a clear day either early in the morning or at sunset "when the shallow grooves cast shadows which help define and outline the shapes."

Oak Island's Money Pit

Eighteen-year-old Daniel McGinnis would no doubt be surprised to know that his discovery of a strange depression on the ground in south-eastern Nova Scotia's Oak Island back in 1795 led to a mystery that continues to baffle visitors and residents to this day. The young man had heard rumours that a pirate ship had been spotted in Mahone Bay; some suggested the infamous Blackbeard hid some of his treasure in the area. McGinnis was on a casual hunt to see if there was any truth to the stories when he discovered the depressed land. He also found a tree branch that looked worn where the limb joined the tree trunk, as if someone had used it as part of a pulley system.

Of course, the discovery got him digging. He and some friends dug until they happened upon a layer of logs about 3 metres down. They removed the logs and continued digging until they came upon another layer of logs another 3 metres below. The pattern repeated until the young men reached the 9-metre mark. At that point they realized they were facing a much larger project than they had first anticipated, and they called it quits, opting to return at a later time with better equipment.

Eight years passed before McGinnis returned to his dig site. This time he had more equipment and more men to help him. The pit continued with its strange layers of earth and oak logs, and as the men dug deeper they also found flagstone and even coconut fibre. At the 27-metre mark the crew uncovered a stone that had what looked as if it had a coded inscription on it. Although there is some debate about the accuracy of the translation, it allegedly reads: "Forty feet below two million pounds are buried."

Buoyed on by the discovery, McGinnis and his crew continued their dig. However, repeated flooding of what was now being called the Money Pit eventually put an end to their efforts.

Further expeditions to the area have resulted in more extensive digging and unveiled additional strange discoveries, along with a series of booby traps. At least six men have died trying to discover the treasure of Oak Island's Money Pit and finally answer the mystery that has remained buried there for more than 200 years. Local legends suggest another death is necessary before the secret behind the mystery is revealed.

Most recently, Michigan brothers Marty and Rick Lagina have purchased the property and poured even more cash into the Money Pit in their ongoing quest for answers. Their efforts are being chronicled in the History Channel program, *The Curse of Oak Island*.

Is there anything in the uncooperative pit on Oak Island? Could it be that Blackbeard's treasure is hidden beneath the layers of booby-traps? Could it contain gold coins hidden during times of war, or is it the impenetrable vault housing Marie Antoinette's missing jewels? Or is the whole site nothing more than a weird hoax?

Amid the many unanswered questions, one thing is certain—despite all the modern technology at our fingertips, Oak Island and its Money Pit represent one of Canada's most baffling mysteries.

Bayer's Lake Mystery Walls

Oak Island isn't the only Nova Scotia location with a weird and mysterious past. In the 1980s as the Bayers Lake area of Halifax was being developed into a business park, workers noticed a stone wall of varying heights bordering a high ridge and snaking its way about 150 metres into the bush. On further exploration east of the walls, in the Chain Lakes Watershed area, two five-sided foundations, the smaller of which included a stone staircase, were also discovered. The problem is that there is no record of these structures. In fact, building in the area had been prohibited since 1846, because the area was where the city managed its water supply.

On its discovery, it was clear the people of Nova Scotia had a bona fide mystery on their hands—one that had considerable history to it. According to the Nova Scotia Archaeology Society, the walls could date back to the 1700s, but there is no evidence to suggest what the structures were built for or by whom. Still, there is archaeological significance to the find, and the provincial government placed the area under the Special Places Protection Act—a piece of legislation that provides for the "preservation, regulation and study of archaeological and historical remains and paleontological and ecological sites."

In the meantime, specialists from the Halifax Regional Municipality and St. Mary's University have investigated the walls and voiced their opinions about the ruins. The most popular theory is that the structures were either used in military training exercises to prepare for storming the Fortress of Louisbourg in 1758, or were "part of an actual defence network for Halifax in the War of 1812." That said, there is no proof that either of these theories is correct—one would expect a record of the site to exist on file somewhere if the area had been built and used for formal military exercises.

Another, less likely, explanation from mystery enthusiasts suggests a connection to the search for the Holy Grail of King Arthur legend. Stranger still is the idea that the walls were erected by alien beings.

In time, researchers might discover the final piece of the puzzle that explains the origins and purpose of the Baker's Lake Mystery Walls. For now, the protected area will tantalize the imagination of visitors and residents alike, and its buildings stand as just another strange structure some people at some point in time decided to build.

Point me to the Money

Listen up, all you treasure hunters. If you've done your rounds at all the popular Canadian hotspots promising buried caches of varying descriptions, there's a lesser-known hideaway said to house an as of yet undetermined treasure.

BUILD IT AND THEY WILL COME

There's been a lot of speculation on the subject, but no one knows what's buried at Money Point, a little blip along the Atlantic coast not far from the ghost town of Ireland's Eye, located at the southwest end of Trinity Bay in Newfoundland and Labrador. At the site, a strange pile of rocks that look to be purposely stacked to mark the location of something important has kept locals wondering for decades.

What makes this pile of rocks different from, say, an Inuksuk stacked by a wilderness hiker is the fact that the pile reappears the day after someone dismantles it to try and uncover what might be buried beneath it.

No one has any idea how the rocks are restacked or by whom. Perhaps it is the local residents secretly trying to keep the mystery alive, restacking the piles should they find the site disrupted.

As for any real treasure—well, that's another mystery. No one has ever come forward to officially report any findings. And even treasure hunters with metal detectors have searched the area and come up empty.

DID YOU KNOW?

The Ireland's Eye Money Point isn't the only Money Point that's said to hide some kind of pirate treasure. There are at least three others. One is located in County Cork, Ireland, another in Chesapeake, Virginia, and the third is near Ingonish, Nova Scotia. It could be said that gold seekers at the Ingonish Money Point had a little more luck finding something valuable. Legend suggests that a fortune in gold coins was dumped into the ocean during the sinking of a French galleon, and that lucky passersby have, on occasion, pocketed the odd gold coin or two that washed ashore after being coughed up by the ocean.

PLACE NAMES, STRANGE SIGNS AND ROADSIDE ATTRACTIONS

PUTTING OUR STAMP ON IT

Our hopes are high. Our faith in the people is great. Our courage is strong. And our dreams for this beautiful country will never die.

–Pierre Trudeau

By the time a community reaches town status in this country it's a given that, should you tour its main street, you'll come across a gas station, burger joint or coffee shop, a store or two, perhaps a civic building or doctor's office, a school or some assortment of the aforementioned. While necessary to our survival, and something most of us look for in the locations where we choose to live, these amenities don't say much about the personality of a place. What does speak volumes, however, are the little extras you come across, such as the UFO landing pad in St. Paul, Alberta. I mean, not everyone can say they live in a community that welcomes everyone, aliens included, with open arms.

From sea to shining sea, Canadians have put their own stamp on their communities with unique roadside attractions. Some are lovely tributes to the natural wonders or human history of a place. Others are more eccentric, such as the world's largest hockey stick and puck in Duncan. But strange statues aren't the only clues to a community's personality. What kind of folks live in Punkeydoodles Corners or Saint-Louis-du-Ha! Ha!, Québec?

From strange road signs to giant mosquitoes, the special flavour of this country and its residents are evident just about everywhere you turn.

Stone Guides

The dictionary defines an inuksuk as, "something which acts for or performs the function of a person" or "inuk" (person) "suk" (substitute). The inuksuk is closely associated with the Inuit culture and was used as a landmark for hunters and trappers to find their way back home on a land that otherwise had few markings. (We Canadians may frown when folks south of the border suggest we live in the frigid north, but we can't argue that a good chunk of our country, north of 60, has flat patches of land covered in snow for most of the year.) The inuksuk is such an important part of the northern culture that the structure was chosen as the central figure of Nunavut's flag.

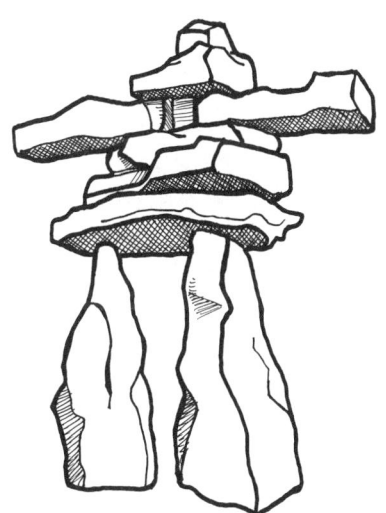

While the simple, attractive structure is not odd or strange to just about anyone living in this country, it is uniquely Canadian. And to celebrate this Canadiana, a 4.5-metre tall inuksuk was designed by an artist named Joe Nattar and built by a crew of Inuit workers in downtown Rankin Inlet in 1991.

Mosquito Haven?

Anyone who's spent a summer in this country can attest to the fact that mosquitoes are an ever-present, and very pesky, reality. But there are some Canadian communities that have decided, for whatever bizarre reason, to pay tribute to this overbearing critter by choosing the mosquito as their roadside attraction!

First up is Mozzy the Mosquito, who welcomes folks to Rainbow Lake, Alberta. This community mascot is perfectly suited to "oil country," being constructed from a modified pump jack. Mozzy overlooks the Rainbow Lake golf course.

Upsala, Ontario, also chose the mosquito as its community mascot. If you've ever been to Ontario in summer, you'll no doubt agree that the residents in this unincorporated community, located smack dab in the middle of Ontario's fishing country, have to share the space with mosquitoes—or rather, the mosquitoes tell them to move over. With that in mind, it's hard to argue against Upsala's decision to use a mosquito mascot to greet folks to their neck of the woods. Although it's gigantic, this mascot is a little more true to life than its Alberta counterpart. The addition of a knife and fork attached to the mosquito's legs, and the entire structure carrying over the likeness of a frightened man, drive home the fact that these pests are out for blood…just in case you had any doubt.

Finally, if you've lived in Manitoba you might argue that they make them skeeters bigger and meaner in this province, especially if you live in Komarno. Not only does a mosquito stand guard at the entrance to this prairie community, it's touted as the "world's biggest mosquito." Not sure if Upsala or Rainbow Lake agree with the claim, but even if they think their rendition of the pesky creature is bigger and better, Komarno can toss out another convincing bit of trivia that make its mosquito claim unique. The name Komarno quite literally means, "mosquito infested" in Ukrainian. (I'm Ukrainian and from Manitoba, and I didn't have a clue!) Furthermore, this community hails itself as the "Mosquito Capital of the World." I bet you're just itching to pack your bags and move on in, eh?

Gophers Galore?

As long as we're on the subject of critters, why not take a quick jaunt to the hamlet of Torrington, Alberta, located 160 kilometres northeast of Calgary. This community, with a population just short of 200 people, has one very large and impressive resident in the form of a 3.6-metre-tall gopher statue named Clem T. GoFur. In addition, Torrington's desire to elevate the gopher to almost human status culminated in the creation of the Gopher Hole Museum in 1996. Since then, the museum has welcomed guests from June to

September every year to visit their little, stuffed gopher dioramas (the critters in anthropomorphic settings). And if a museum dedicated to these varmints wasn't tribute enough, all 11 fire hydrants in the small community have been painted to look like, you guessed it, gophers!

DID YOU  KNOW?

Not all gophers are created equal. Pocket gophers are the only "true" gophers, but they have distant ground squirrel relatives that are colloquially known as gophers. The gophers at the Gopher Hole Museum are actually Richardson's ground squirrels.

Gainer the Gopher, the official mascot of the Saskatchewan Roughriders, is another ground squirrel masquerading as a gopher. He's been leading the cheering section for Roughrider fans since 1977 and he isn't showing any signs of slowing down! I guess "Gainer the Ground Squirrel" isn't as catchy.

Sweep! Sweep!

The folks down in Arborg, Manitoba, take the sport of curling seriously. The town first organized a curling team back in 1945, and the local high school earned three provincial championship titles in the sport—in 1948, 1949 and 1988. Since then the community's love for curling has continued to grow, and to commemorate their love of the sport, in June 2005 the town erected the world's largest curling rock.

PLACE NAMES, STRANGE SIGNS AND ROADSIDE ATTRACTIONS

ALL IN A NAME

Rat Portage

Kenora is truly one of Canada's best-kept secrets. The remote city is located on the northern portion of beautiful Lake of the Woods and offers the best in all-season sports. But it didn't always go by the name Kenora. In 1878, when a permanent settlement was first established there, it was known as Wauzhushk Onigum, a First Nations term roughly translated as "portage to the country of the muskrat," which then became Rat Portage. The community adopted the name "Kenora" in 1905 by using the first two letters in Keewaitin, (a community just east of Kenora), Norman (once a separate community that was enveloped by Kenora and is now the neighbourhood of Norman) and Rat Portage. Come to think of it, Rat Portage may have been a strange name but the name's evolution to Kenora is even more unique!

All You Need is Love

Leading the way when it comes to unique place names with a, shall we say, uniquely friendly twist is Newfoundland and Labrador. We can begin with Come by Chance, Heart's Content, Heart's Delight and Heart's Desire and work our way up to Little Heart's Ease and Little Paradise, not to mention Spread Eagle, Dildo and Conception Bay. Now if you're looking for information about where these names came from, let me suggest it might be more fun to just let your imagination roam.

Inside Joke

A scant 35 kilometres south of St. John's, Newfoundland, is the tourist hub of Witless Bay. Local folklore suggests the first group of Europeans to settle in the area included a man named Captain Whittle and his family, and so the area was named Whittle's Bay in their honour. Now I know what you're thinking. There's a difference between Whittle and Witless, but just hear me out. In a sad turn of events, the dear Captain Whittle died, leaving his widow to raise their children alone. The daunting task left the young woman wanting to return to family in her native Dorsetshire, England. With all the Whittles gone, the name Whittle's Bay evolved into Whittles-less Bay and, eventually, Witless Bay (or so the story goes).

Good Luck Prevails

The word swastika doesn't stir up warm fuzzies for most of us. But for the people of Swastika, Ontario, it's not only the name they're used to—it's one they fought to keep. "Swastika" comes from the Sanskrit word for "well being" or "good fortune," and the associated symbol has long stood as a symbol of success and good fortune to people of the Hindu, Buddhist and Jainism faiths. When James and William Dusky staked their claim along nearby Otto Lake and founded the Swastika Gold Mine, good fortune indeed flowed. As the mine thrived, a community of the same name blossomed, and it was incorporated in 1908.

However, world events would soon cast a pall on the community's choice of name. With the advent of World War II, and the use of a swastika as a symbol for Hitler's Third Reich, the word swastika no longer evoked feelings of good fortune, and the provincial government proposed a name change to Winston. In fact, they took down the Swastika signs and replaced them with Winston signs. But the residents of Swastika would have none of it. They tore down the new signs and replaced them with their originals, along with an added commentary: "To hell with Hitler, we came up with our name first!"

DID YOU KNOW?

Ontario once had another community with a German connection—Berlin, Ontario. Around the time of World War I, a name change was proposed, and residents, though divided, were not quite as opposed to the idea as those in Swastika would prove to be. So in 1912, Berlin changed its name to Kitchener.

Enduring Mystery

I bet you'd like to know where the community name Ecum Secum came from.

Sorry to disappoint, but the best I can do is share with you the confusion and conjecture I discovered during my hours of research, although I have no doubt that someone reading this entry will dig up my contact information and enlighten me. In the meantime, a book entitled *Nova Scotia,* of the Moon Travel Guides series, suggests the name is actually a "Mi'kmaq word of unknown origin." Wikipedia, however, suggests the term translates to "red house," which to my mind leaves more questions than answers.

Love Those Libations

Apparently there was once a place named Community Punch Bowl in Alberta, but time has not been kind to this town, and it seems to have disappeared completely. (Perhaps it drank its way into oblivion?) There is, however, a Punch Bowl Falls near Jasper.

Milk River, named after its founders' belief that they had indeed found the land of "milk and honey," has fared better through the years and continues to thrive. Whiskey Gap, on the other hand, might have attracted residents with a taste for the hard stuff back during Alberta's Prohibition, when it acted as a kind of underground railway for those not wanting to go cold turkey. But today little remains, and the only official listing for Whiskey Gap is on Alberta's list of ghost towns.

East Coast Paradise

There's a little less confusion over the naming of Garden of Eden, Nova Scotia. Early immigrants William Alexander MacDonald and his family were among the first settlers of this community, and they gave the town its name. To my way of thinking the MacDonalds must have believed the peaceful surroundings to be a newfound paradise after their long journey from Scotland. In fact, they loved it so much there are still descendants of the original MacDonald settlers living in the community.

Stop! Thief!

Chances are that if you didn't know where you were going, you might just miss Punkeydoodles Corners altogether. Most folks, in fact, have probably never heard of it. But those folks that do manage to stumble across the Ontario hamlet love its name, and many have absconded with its sign. Who wouldn't want the sign "Punkeydoodles Corners" hanging in their man cave?

As to the origin of the name, there is no shortage of theories. Some stories refer to a local innkeeper who loved singing "Yankee Doodle," but must have talked with some kind of accent or impediment because it sounded to patrons more like "punkey doodle." Others have suggested the word is rooted in Victorian English and means to waste time. Still others posit the name was gifted to a "lazy pumpkin farmer" by his frustrated spouse.

Unique Claim to Fame

The origin of the Québec community's name Saint-Louis-du-Ha! Ha! includes reference to people (it's uncertain if it refers to one or all of three community shakers named Louis at the time of its founding), as well as its geographic location. But the most interesting part about this place name isn't necessarily where the name came from but rather it's claim to fame as the "only town in the world with two exclamation points in its name." Now if that doesn't put a smile on your face I don't know what will.

No Mystery Here

You've got to admit that on first hearing the name Crotch Lake, Ontario, you might wonder why someone would have chose to christen this pristine wilderness with such an, well, awkward name. I couldn't find a trustworthy reference suggesting where the name came from, but before you bury your head too deep in the gutter, let me tell you what I did find out. I decided to go back to basics and look up "crotch" in the dictionary. Did you know that the official definition of the word is "a forking or place of forking, as of the human body between the legs?" Take that a step further and look on a map, and one can see how this lake has several areas that can be described as a "place of forking," so I suggest the name Crotch Lake fits very well indeed!

Pride in our Nation

Adanac, Saskatchewan, once a growing community with a store, school and other typical amenities, is today a little hamlet that some websites have taken to refer to as a ghost town. In 2009, a SaskHealth report listed an official population of just two people, but the name of this fading community is as large and patriotic as one can get. Adanac is simply Canada spelled backwards.

PLACE NAMES, STRANGE SIGNS AND ROADSIDE ATTRACTIONS

YOU WANT ME TO DO WHAT?

City of Champions?

Pranksters had fun adding a placard reading "Road Construction City," to the City of Edmonton's welcome sign. To maintain Edmonton's status as the "City of Champions," the placard was quickly removed, but not before those responsible for the prank snapped a few pictures and posted them on the Internet. The placard was followed up with another in the fall of 2013. It read, "City of Speed Traps." That sign didn't last much longer, but it too made Internet news as a photo on Canada.ca.

DID YOU  KNOW?

Not sure if I'm alone in this, but I always thought Edmonton was nicknamed the "City of Champions" because of the Edmonton Oilers' five-year run at winning the Stanley Cup, not to mention the Edmonton Eskimos—the Eskies have 13 Grey Cups to their credit. But I was wrong. Former mayor Laurence Decore uttered the phrase in 1987 after the residents of Edmonton and surrounding areas experienced an F4 tornado that claimed 27 lives and caused millions of dollars in damage. The phrase eventually moved from a cursory comment to the media to become the city's official slogan.

Dog Loving City

This sign comes to you courtesy of the dog-loving civic leaders from the District of North Vancouver. Echoing bylaw

5981-11(i), the sign reads: "Attention Dog Guardians. Pick up after your dogs. Thank you. Attention Dogs: Grrr, bark, woof. Good dog."

Read the Fine Print

This sign in North Vancouver flashes "CAUTION" in large letters before stating, "This sign has SHARP EDGES. Do not touch the edges of this sign." Strange, wouldn't you agree? Stranger still is what's written in small letters below: "Also, the bridge is out ahead." Gives testament to the advice to read the fine print.

Wildlife Ahead

This sign warns of the potential to meet local wildlife when driving along a particular (but unnamed) stretch of road near Bancroft, Ontario. Deer, you might think? Or moose? Think again. The kind of creature you might meet here wouldn't put a dent in your car but, should you carelessly drive by, you'd likely flatten it. This sign sports a picture of a turtle, with a 2-kilometre speed limit between May and September.

Animal Cruelty?

We all know that feeding wildlife our food isn't good for the animals. So perhaps this sign from the Yukon shouldn't come as a surprise. Attached to a wire fence was the picture of a hand, circled and crossed out in red, followed by the words, "PLEASE do not feed fingers to the animals."

A SHORT COURSE IN CANADIAN HISTORY

Canada is a country whose main exports are hockey players and cold fronts. Our main imports are baseball players and acid rain.

—Pierre Trudeau

Don't panic! I'm not about to rewrite the history books here. But there are a lot of cool bits of Canadiana that are often overlooked in the history portion of our country's school curriculum. For example, did you know our anthem was composed by Calixa Lavallee, and the original lyrics were in French, written by Adolphe-Basile Routhier? The song was called "Chant National" and was first performed in Quebec City in 1880. Many versions with English lyrics followed; the English lyrics as we know them today were based on a version penned in 1908 by Mr. Justice Robert Stanley Weir. "O Canada" was officially adopted as our nation's anthem in July 1, 1980.

Read on and you'll discover other equally interesting tidbits.

A Loonie Story

It appears the Canadian government had different design plans for their dollar coin back in the 1980s when it first came into circulation as a cost-saving measure to replace the dollar bill. Apparently the original design sported the image of a voyageur, not a loon. But the master dies went missing during transportation to Winnipeg in November of 1986, and so it was back to the drawing board to create a new design, resulting in the Canadian loonie we all know and love.

While the loonie officially replaced the dollar bill in 1987, the first silver dollar ever minted in Canada rolled off the assembly line in 1935 to celebrate the 25th anniversary of George V's coronation.

DID YOU KNOW?

The Royal Canadian Mint made it into the Guinness World Records in 2007 after minting the largest coin in the world—a "100 kg, 99.999% pure $1 million gold bullion coin." According to the Canadian Mint's official website, five such coins have been minted to date, and each was purchased by private investors.

Trudeau Legacy

Pierre Trudeau is arguably the most popular Canadian prime minister of recent times, a fact supported by his recognition in December 1999 as the "top Canadian newsmaker of the 20th century." He loved women and dated celebrities like Barbara Streisand and Liona Boyd. He was as daring as he was clever. But most of all, he was so charismatic that his leap into politics took him from earning his seat in the 1965 federal election to his nomination as a candidate for the leadership of the Liberal Party just three years later. When he won that challenge, he called an election and won that battle, too. By then, Trudeaumania was born. People started to take an interest in politics because of Trudeau's approach and delivery, which, some biographers have suggested, made it "cool."

Trudeau also had a familial connection to several other famous Trudeaus, including American cartoonist Garry Trudeau of *Doonesbury* fame. The two men were related through an early French settler named Etienne Trudeau (1641–1712). In fact, the book *Ghost Empire: How the French Almost Conquered North America* stated, "virtually every person named Trudeau in North America" is Etienne's descendant.

When his divorce from Margaret Sinclair became final in 1984, Pierre Trudeau made history as the first Canadian Prime Minister who also had the role of a single parent. Trudeau was also a second-degree black belt in the Japanese martial art of sho-dan when he retired from politics that same year.

Cats on Guard

Canadians with a fondness for felines might find it interesting to learn that Parliament Hill was once home to a cat sanctuary. Cats were first brought to The Hill in 1924 in an effort to curb the mouse problem or, as one author put it, rid the newly constructed Centre Block of the "mild plague of rats and mice" that had taken up residence there.

The cats brought on board to deal with the rodent population weren't spayed or neutered, and before long there were dozens of stray cats living behind Centre Block. This, of course, necessitated additional chores for the custodians on staff, who took on the responsibility of feeding and caring for the animals.

More modern methods of dealing with mice and rats eventually caught on in the country's capital, and by the 1950s the powers that manage the our federal buildings no longer relied on cats to deal with their rat problems. However, the cats were there, and even with the establishment of a colony and the building of shelters, it wasn't hard for those visiting the grounds to come across one of the frisky critters. After all, cats aren't easily confined and can tackle even the tallest fences, and it seemed the public didn't mind sharing the grounds with the furry critters. In fact, the cat colony became quite the tourist draw.

Of course, lawmakers can't enact legislation without following through in their own right. So the cats in the sanctuary were not only fed and sheltered, but also vetted and, eventually, spayed and neutered, which is what most municipalities expect of their resident cat owners. However, even with donations of food from Purina and gifts of free examinations and vaccinations by a local vet, by 2003 the roughly 30 cats still living at the Hill cost Canadian taxpayers upwards of $6000 every year.

But the era of Parliamentary cats was not to be forever. By 2012, it was harder for visitors to spy one of the four remaining Parliamentary Cats. And in 2013, these last four cats were captured and adopted out, and the structures originally built for them were dismantled.

DID YOU  KNOW?

Visitors to our nation's capital may not have formed any firm opinions about our system of government, but if noted Canadian author, television personality and journalist Pierre Berton was right in his estimation, as many as 300 visitors toured the cat sanctuary on nice days. In fact, media outlets around the world reported stories of the cat sanctuary; questions about the Parliamentary cats even made it onto a Japanese game show.

Hot Shots

Historically speaking, lacrosse, not hockey, has always been Canada's official sport. Lacrosse earned that title in 1859, but despite its long history most Canadians don't know much about the game, much less play it themselves. Hockey, on the other hand…well, just about everyone knows about hockey, and most folks have played some rendition of the sport, even if it's just shooting a rubber ball around the living room with a miniature plastic stick. In Canada, hockey represents Saturday night family time around the TV, with potato chips and beer nearby. It's an institution, for pity sake! And its lack of status must have caused enough irritation that eventually the powers that be decided to do something about it. So on May 12, 1994, the National Sports of Canada Act recognized hockey as the country's national winter sport and lacrosse as Canada's national summer sport.

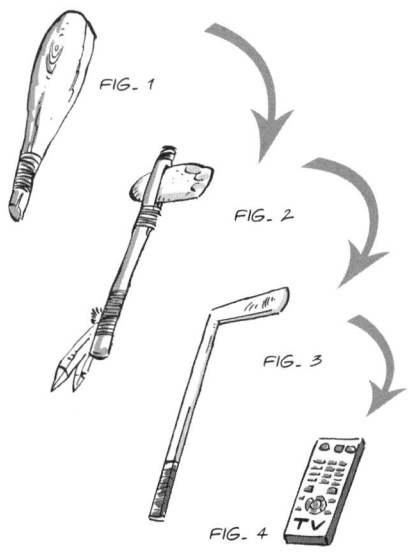

DID YOU KNOW?

Less than 11 percent of this country's land is owned privately. The remaining 89 percent is owned as follows: 41 percent belongs to the federal government and the provinces own the remaining 48 percent.

The Devil's in the Details

When the Bank of Canada released it's newest set of paper notes in 1954, they were no doubt proud of the collection. Featured on the bills was a picture of the newly crowned Queen Elizabeth based on a photograph taken by the internationally renowned Canadian, Yousuf Karsh. What a beautiful queen she is, too! However, once the bills were released some folks saw something rather sinister. In particular, the hair behind the young queen's ear was said to give "the illusion of a grinning demon." The series of bills that year became known as the "Devil's Head" or "Devil's Face" series. And if you're lucky enough to have a few of these bills tucked away, you might be in for another surprise. According to the Bank of Canada, a $1 Devil's Face note is worth between $5 and $75 dollars, depending on its condition.

MARITIME MYSTERIES

WATER, WATER EVERYWHERE

The world is full of obvious things which nobody by any chance ever observes.

–Arthur Conan Doyle

The National Oceanic and Atmospheric Administration, based in Silver Springs, Maryland, is on record as suggesting that although the ocean covers more than 70 percent of the earth's surface, less than five percent has been explored. Perhaps that's why almost every civilization through time with a connection to the ocean (or other bodies of water) has legends about it. With more than 200,000 kilometres of shoreline surrounding this country, which also contains about one-fifth of the world's freshwater supply, it's no surprise we have a fair number of mysteries and legends of our own.

Woeful Record

A simple cairn located on Spencer's Island, Nova Scotia, reads, "Nearby the world's most famous mystery ship, the *Mary Celeste*, a brigantine, was built and launched in 1861. Was first named the *Amazon*. In 1868 she was driven ashore in a storm and after being repaired was renamed the *Mary Celeste*. In December 1872 she was discovered at sea with all sails set and everything in order. But not a person was on board or ever found."

The *Mary Celeste* was built smack dab in the middle of Canada's shipbuilding heyday. Unfortunately the ship's first few years were anything but positive. Originally christened the *Amazon*, the ship wasn't at all kind to its first three captains. One might go so far as to suggest the vessel was cursed.

Robert McLellan, captain number one, reportedly died of pneumonia just a week after setting sail on the ship's maiden voyage. Captain number two, John Nutting Parker, died in a fire that broke out when the *Amazon* was anchored at a shipyard for repairs caused by its collision with a fishing boat. Captain number three may not have died, but he didn't fare much better: he was fired after his ship collided with another ship near Dover.

They say bad luck comes in threes, and it seemed like the ship's streak of bad luck was finally over. For the next few years she hauled cargo without major mishap. But in 1867, the ship hit stormy seas and ran aground on the Atlantic coast near Glace Bay, Nova Scotia.

At this point, an American named Richard Haines of New York purchased and repaired the *Amazon*. The ship was renamed the *Mary Celeste* after it was transferred to the American registry. Captain Benjamin Spooner Briggs, one of the ship's shareholders and a man of considerable experience, took the helm on November 5, 1872. Accompanied by his wife, Sarah, and two-year-old daughter, Sophia, Briggs planned to leave Staten Island harbour with a cargo of 1701 barrels of commercial alcohol. He and his crew of seven were headed out to Genoa, Italy.

On either December 4 or 5, depending on the source, the *Mary Celeste* was discovered drifting some 644 kilometres east of the Azores. No one was on board, and none of the ship's crew or passengers was ever found.

Had everyone just abandoned ship? And if so, why?

Because valuable personal belongings were still aboard, along with the barrels of alcohol, it was doubtful that the ship suffered a pirate attack. Some suggested the crew mutinied, killing Briggs and his family before escaping on the lifeboat—one of the few things missing from the ship. That theory seemed unlikely: everyone on board appeared to have stellar reputations and, again, nothing of value was missing.

An examination of the ship and its cargo provide more questions than answers. Of the 1701 barrels of alcohol on board, nine were empty. Was it possible, as some suggested, that the crew consumed the missing alcohol and did away with Briggs and his family in a drunken stupor? Again, there didn't seem to be any reason for such behaviour.

One of the most promising theories was posited by a 2007 Smithsonian television documentary. It suggested that Briggs ordered his family and crew to abandon ship sometime on November 25, the day of his last entry on the ship's slate, after discovering one of his bilge pumps was plugged and erroneously deducing the ship was in danger of sinking. According to Briggs' last notation, the *Mary Celeste* was less than 10 kilometres from shore. If the captain thought the threat great enough, he would have certainly protected those in his care by lowering the lifeboat, reasoning they should have no problems making their way to shore.

Sadly, the lifeboat didn't make it to safety, but the *Mary Celeste* made it considerably farther than 10 kilometres, albeit in the wrong direction. With such evidence of its seaworthiness, the *Mary Celeste* would have certainly completed its original journey safely had everyone remained on board. Instead, the Mary Celeste has gone down in history as one of this Canada's biggest maritime mysteries.

One for the Weird File

Imagine thinking your father, a ship's captain, died when the schooner he manned sank during heavy storms. Then out of the blue, 10 years later, someone calls from another country, 2000 kilometres away, to tell you your father just died? That's exactly what happened when Horace Smith of Toronto, Ontario, received a telegram from Harrah, Oklahoma, on March 27, 1927, saying the body of his newly deceased father was being held for him to claim.

Captain John W. Smith was manning the schooner, the *George A. Marsh,* when it sank in Lake Ontario on August 17, 1917. Twelve of the 14 crew and passengers died in the disaster; Smith, his wife and six of his children were among them. The problem was, the bodies of all 12 deceased were recovered with the exception of John W. Smith, leading some to believe that he may have survived. In light of the news from Oklahoma, some went so far as to say Smith had been living south of the border all that time, possibly off the bounty of a treasure some rumoured had been sunk near Oswego, Ontario.

Those who were closest to him, including his son Horace, argued that the suggestion John W. Smith deserted them was ridiculous. In fact, it was tantamount to suggesting the man murdered his family!

In case the ridiculous nature of this story hasn't totally convinced you that people on all fronts were going far beyond any reasonable connection, ask yourself this: is it possible the name John Smith was as common back in 1927 as it is today, and if so, how many other men shared that name between Ontario and Oklahoma?

Fated Expedition Still a Mystery

From the late 15th century, European leaders financed expeditions seeking a northern shortcut from their shores to Asia, and with every expedition more lands were charted, more information discovered. But by 1845, almost three centuries later, the shortcut remained elusive, so British Admiral Sir John Barrow decided to organize one last expedition before retiring from service. Barrow was a great proponent of Arctic exploration and had a wealth of experience under his belt, but as he entered his eighth decade he had yet to accomplish—or witness the accomplishment—of the discovery of a Northwest Passage.

Barrow secured the HMS *Erebus* and HMS *Terror*, and chose Sir John Franklin to command the journey from Lancaster Sound through the 1670 kilometres of frigid, iceberg-ridden waters of the Arctic Ocean, to China. Truth be told, Franklin wasn't Barrow's first choice of commanding officer. Both James Fitzjames, who captained the HMS *Erebus,* and Francis Crozier, who stood at the helm of the HMS *Terror,* were considered for Franklin's role but were discounted for various reasons. And so Barrow reluctantly decided to go with Franklin. The two ships used in the voyage were sturdily built and were reinforced with the latest technology. They carried a four-year supply of food, 1200 books and even a player piano to ensure the crew of 129 men wouldn't suffer the loss of creature comforts with their extended voyage.

At least that was the plan.

The expedition left the safety of the harbour at Greenhithe, England, on May 19, 1845. The crews of two whalers, the *Prince of Wales* and the *Enterprise*, were the last to see the ships of the Franklin expedition, in late July of the same year, as they all waited for favourable sailing conditions near

Lancaster Sound. A few short months later, Franklin and his men wintered on Beechey Island, proceeding the following spring. Then in September 1846, both ships under Franklin's command became trapped in ice near King William Island.

Franklin and his crew weren't initially worried, according to the only document ever discovered from the voyage. It stated that although their ships had gotten stuck in the ice off King William Island, all was well. But nothing could be further from the truth, and a postscript added to the document reported that Franklin died on June 11, 1847. The following spring any remaining survivors set out on foot, looking for the nearest outpost. Investigators generally believed the ships never sailed again, although one Inuit community reported that one of the ships tried to venture south, perhaps making it to Queen Maud Gulf or Wilmot and Crampton Bay.

Regardless, in the end, no one from either ship survived.

Bits and pieces of the expedition and several skeletal remains have been discovered over the past 170 years by explorers looking for an answer to whatever became of the men manning the damned mission. Many theories have emerged, including that the men succumbed to a combination of lead poisoning and scurvy. More recent studies suggest it's likely the men died of a combination of bad luck and poor preparation, coupled with a stubborn disregard for the customs and teachings of the Inuit people who knew the land and the best way to survive the extreme conditions.

Clues Slow in Coming

Whatever became of the HMS *Erebus* and HMS *Terror*? Scientific explorations looking for answers about their fate and that of their crews have been ongoing since 1982, but every year those expeditions end with few, if any, results. In

September 2014, the CBC reported that, about 1200 square kilometres, or half the area targeted as the most likely resting place for the two vessels had been searched without so much as an anchor uncovered. And then a few weeks after that report, nearing the end of the 2014 search, the *Erebus* was finally discovered with a remote underwater vehicle owned by Parks Canada.

DID YOU KNOW?

Norway Captain Roald Amundsen successfully navigated the Northwest Passage in 1906. Despite his successful journey, the passage was deemed an unsafe route for European merchants to take on their way to the exotic shores of Asia to trade their wares.

Mysterious Discovery

There are an estimated 4700 shipwrecks littering the Great Lakes, about 550 of which are believed to be in Lake Ontario. So it's not a big surprise when, from time to time, modern-day treasure hunters discover a wreck.

But in the fall of 2008, a discovery by Jim Kennard and Dan Scoville was definitely more of a surprise than most. The two men discovered a rare 19th century, 55-foot long daggerboard ship. The wood-panel ship is the only one of its kind that has been discovered in the Great Lakes, but what's truly strange is that there are no records of such a vessel sinking in Lake Ontario. And despite the fact that Kennard and Scoville examined the ship further with the help of a remote operated vehicle equipped to photograph the wreck, they were unable to discover its name. The ship, lodged on the lake bottom more than 152 metres below the surface, remained remarkably intact. At the same time, the ship looked to be stripped of anything of value, including its anchors and iron fittings—and, perhaps, its name?

In May of the same year, Kennard and Scoville made another one-of-a-kind discovery when they located the British warship HMS *Ontario*. The ship was reported lost in 1780, making it the oldest shipwreck found to date in the Great Lakes and the sole British warship dating from that period in the world.

THE COMPLEXITIES OF BEING CANADIAN

PUZZLING PEOPLE AND THEIR PERPLEXING STORIES

Canadians can easily "pass for American" as long as we don't accidentally use metric measurements or apologize when hit by a car.

–Douglas Coupland

Just like people make a house a home, it's the Canadian people who really make this country unique. Sure there are the crankpots among us, but for the most part we're a happy lot. We are known for our hospitality, and we proudly proclaim it—Manitoba boasts the fact with its "Friendly Manitoba" license plate. We're inclined to apologize when someone bumps into us at the grocery store (at least I am). And when we leave the supermarket with more money than we should have, we return to customer service to explain that we've been undercharged. (Okay, so maybe that's just me, but my excuse for that behaviour is that I'm a polite Canadian. And did I mention Canadians value honesty?)

We Canadians love our coffee, and the chance to share it with someone. We're generous to a fault and tolerant of different viewpoints, religions and lifestyles. We believe in personal freedoms, and we try to recognize the good in our neighbours, even when we really don't understand where they're coming from.

Of course all this personal freedom gives us a lot of room for experimentation, for stretching our wings and trying new things. So with every ordinary Canadian you meet, there's another with a quirk or eccentricity that will surprise you to the moon and back. You'll find folks who live in shoe houses and politicians who've had their hand in top-secret activities of the alien research kind, or a man who investigates strange animal mutilations and a University professor who believes he has discovered a way to "talk" to animals.

Meteghan's Mystery Man

Some of us couldn't keep a secret if our life depended on it. And then there are people that, no matter how hard you try, you can't pull a secret out of them.

Meteghan's mystery man, Jerome, seems to fit into the second category.

Truth told, no one knew if Jerome was the real name of the gent discovered near Sandy Cove. The story goes that two fishermen collecting rockweed along the shores of the Bay of Fundy noticed what appeared to be a man huddled against a rock. The man looked to be in his twenties and was fair skinned. His legs were bandaged and appeared to be newly, but professionally, amputated. His clothes were made from fine linens, but he had nothing more than a jug of water and a loaf of bread—or a tin of biscuits, according to some stories—by his side. When the fishermen talked to the man, he responded with grunts. The only three words he seemed able to utter were "Jerome," "Trieste" and "Columbo." People took to calling him Jerome, reasoning that was his name. Some thought Trieste could have referred to a seaport in Italy, and others suggested Columbo might be the name of a ship, but these theories were never proven.

Shocked by the discovery, the people of the rural community of Digby Neck initially cared for Jerome until he was taken to the home of an Italian named Jean Nicolas of Meteghan in 1864. Jerome lived with Nicolas and his family for the next seven years. Because Nicolas spoke five languages, it was believed he had the best chance of getting Jerome to talk. Unfortunately, Jerome either couldn't, or wouldn't, speak.

When Nicolas and his family left Meteghan, Jerome was placed at the home of Didier Comeau of St. Alphonse, where he remained until his passing 42 years later. The provincial government contributed financially to Jerome's care, but the mystery man was also on occasion put on public display, and people paid a fee to see him, not unlike the curiosities that drew crowds to the travelling shows and circuses that became popular in the latter part of the 19th century.

According to the official death registration on file with the Nova Scotia Archives and Records, Jerome succumbed to bronchitis on April 15, 1912, the same day the Titanic sank. He was about 85-years-old.

Tantalized by the tale, amateur and professional sleuths around the world have tried their hands at solving the mystery surrounding Jerome. Some say Jerome was a nobleman of wealthy lineage and was maimed and left for dead by someone wanting to usurp him of his inheritance. Abandoning the man on what was then one of the most isolated regions of the province should have spelled certain death. Others have posited that Jerome might have been an injured naval officer who was no longer worth his keep. Still others suggested pirates captured the man—just uttering the word "pirate" allegedly sent Jerome into a frenzy. And some believed Jerome was actually Jeremiah Mahony, an Irishman who'd immigrated to the United States from Ireland in an effort to get away from his family.

Jerome's death notice in the local newspaper stated, "To all appearances a gentleman, and apparently of European origin, in half a century among the Acadians of the Shore, he could never be induced nor surprised into revealing the slightest clue as to his origin, identity or the cause for his horrible mutilation." Either Jerome chose to maintain his silence, or he was simply unable to communicate the events that occurred to permanently alter the course of his life. Jerome was buried in the Stella Maris Catholic Cemetery, Meteghan, Nova Scotia.

"Everybody thought he was carrying some kind of a secret. There was something he knew and that he was not allowed to say," Comeau told the Halifax Herald in 2000. "After more than 50 years of silence, he died, taking his secret with him to his grave."

Double Take?

Playright Germaine Comeau had yet another theory to explain the Jerome mystery. Comeau suggested Jerome was actually a man from New Brunswick who went by the name of Gamby. Gamby's story was another conundrum. He was discovered, half frozen and covered in snow, by a group of lumberjacks heading home for the Christmas holidays. Gamby was then taken to the nearby village and placed in the care of the Overseers of the Poor of the Parish of Chipman. In the spring of 1861, he contracted gangrene, and like Jerome, had his legs amputated at the knee.

By 1863 the cost of Gamby's care got to be too much for Chipman's residents, so they paid to have him removed from their town. Perhaps they placed him on a ship—maybe even the same strange ship some described as the Spanish warship seen in St. Mary's Bay just before Jerome's discovery. Could

Jerome and Gamby indeed be the same person? The theory seems plausible, but doesn't quite fit with reports that when he was discovered, it was thought that Jerome's legs had been recently amputated.

Mad Trapper of Rat River Still a Mystery

How is it that we can connect with people at different times in their life and yet not ever really know who they really are? Such was the case of the man going by the name of Albert Johnson.

Johnson arrived in Fort MacPherson, Northwest Territories, in the summer of 1931. He was described as a strong man with a stocky build and a cold, unfriendly demeanour. He kept to himself, living in a small cabin he built along the Rat River. He also started trapping in the area, and there was talk that he purposely disturbed traps belonging to other trappers, hoping to steer game in his direction and ultimately fatten his wallet.

As you can imagine, folks in the area became more than a little perturbed with the newcomer and lodged complaints with their neighbourhood Royal Canadian Mounted Police (RCMP). With nothing more than a desire to speak with the man and encourage him to play nice with his neighbours, Constable Alfred King and Special Constable Joe Bernard rode up to Johnson's cabin. Johnson had no interest in discussing anything with the Mounties and steadfastly refused to open his door to them.

The Mounties returned to their constabulary to pick up reinforcements before trying to speak with Johnson again. This time, four Mounties and a civilian made their way to the cabin. Unfortunately, this visit would turn out far worse than the first. When Constable King knocked on Johnson's door, he was greeted with a single gunshot.

Miraculously, King's life was saved. But Johnson's actions set off a series of events that would take the "Mad Trapper of Rat River" and the Mounties tracking him on a five-week journey through treacherous territory in temperatures dipping down to −46°C. And on February 17, 1932, Johnson finally met his end in a hail of gunfire with no less than nine bullets riddling his body.

Although the hunt ended, the mystery surrounding Johnson continues to this day. Who was Albert Johnson? Where did he come from? Had he been on the run from something or someone when he arrived in the north? And why did he have in excess of $2000 and some placer gold in his possession when he died? With these questions unanswered, Johnson is by far one of the strangest individuals in Canadian history.

THE COMPLEXITIES OF BEING CANADIAN

UNIQUE FOLKS AND THEIR TAKE ON LIFE

Changing Course

When he was a boy, his schoolyard friends may have known Archibald Stansfeld Belaney simply as Archie, but as a man he shed that name—and the life that came with it—for a new identity that better matched his new outlook on life.

Belaney was born in England on September 18, 1888. At a young age he developed a keen interest in First Nations culture, and in 1906, he emigrated to Canada under the guise of wanting to study agriculture.

School, however, wasn't where Belaney's heart belonged. Before long he immersed himself in the lifestyle that appealed to him, working as a fur trapper, wilderness guide, and even forest ranger, or "keeper of the animals." Eventually, he settled in the prairies.

Enamoured with the Ojibwe people, Belaney not only adopted their lifestyle and culture, but he also adopted the Ojibwe name Wenjiganooshiinh, which translates roughly to "great grey owl."

For Grey Owl, trapping continued to provide a means of survival, and selling beaver pelts provided good cash. But his views on trapping, and the way he would spend the last, most notable decade of his life, changed when he met a 19-year-old Mohawk woman named Gertrude Bernard. The two fell madly in love.

As with most relationships, everything wasn't a bed of roses. For one thing, Gertrude wasn't happy with Grey Owl trapping beaver. During one hunting trip, when Grey Owl caught a mother beaver, leaving her two kits to cry like human babies from their neighbouring den, Gertrude challenged Grey Owl about his livelihood.

Her challenge didn't stop Grey Owl from selling the mother beaver's pelt, but it must have stirred something in him because he returned the next day and adopted the kits. This adoption signalled a change in his life, as he moved from being a hunter to a conservationist. From then on, until his early death at the age of 49, Grey Owl lobbied to restore the rapidly declining beaver population to its former healthy state and educated the general public about the need for conservation through his numerous articles and books.

A fascinating, somewhat quirky life, wouldn't you agree? But in one area Grey Owl moved from mildly eccentric to one-of-a-kind. I mean, how many conservationists, no matter how focused on their cause, can claim to have raised two young beavers?

DID YOU  KNOW?

Grey Owl named his pet beavers Jelly Roll and Rawhide; archival photos picture the man feeding one of his adoptees a jellyroll, hence the name. One can only speculate where Rawhide got his name.

The cabin where Grey Owl eventually settled his new "family" was located in Prince Albert National Park. Visitors to the park can hike to this cabin and see for themselves how Grey Owl and his family lived. By now I bet you won't be surprised to learn that the cabin was equipped with an indoor beaver dam for the optimal comfort of his two young wards.

Animal Lover

During his later years Fernand Belzil kept himself busy with an extremely rare expertise. Living in the area of St. Paul, Alberta, he was the person farmers would call when they made gruesome animal-related discoveries on their property. I'm not exaggerating here—I'm talking really gruesome. Like animals with their throats ripped open and intestines pulled through, without so much as a footprint on site or a drop of blood splattered in the process.

St. Paul's UFO hotline—and yes, St. Paul has such a thing—was responsible for Belzil's first official call-out, in the mid-1990s. From then on, until his death in 2013, Belzil investigated so many strange animal deaths that even *Maclean's* magazine ran a story on him. And though he wouldn't admit to thinking aliens were responsible for some of the strange sights he'd seen, he did admit to being "a little more accepting of the strange phenomena."

Bizarre animal mutilations were reported more than a century ago in England, but the first case in North America seems to have occurred in Alamosa, Colorado, in 1967, when a three-year-old horse was discovered butchered, her head and neck cleaved to the bone. As with most of these cases, not a drop of blood was found despite the obvious brutality of the scene.

That initial story was in many ways typical of the cases Belzil examined. They were considered "clean kills," meaning the death wasn't the result of a predator. Blood is usually drained from the body and organs are removed with surgical precision. While Belzil didn't offer any concrete theories about what happened to these critters, his exposure to so many scenes with frightening similarities made him a one-of-a-kind expert on the matter.

Talk with the Animals

It's been said that fiction mirrors real life, but sometimes fiction is also responsible for planting the seeds for new research. At least that's the stand I'm going to take on this next entry.

Dr. Ian Duncan, Emeritus Chair in animal welfare at the University of Guelph, made headlines in March 2014 when he outlined his desire to communicate with animals. In particular, Duncan was concerned whether they were "happy with their living conditions and that they were being well cared for." Duncan believes that, like people from different countries, different animal species each have their own unique "language," making the prospect of devising a communications strategy even more difficult than it might at first seem.

According to several journals reporting on Duncan's work, the Scottish-born Canadian professor uses a "strictly scientific method" in devising communication strategies—one that could be used across various species. Specifically, Duncan decided to offer the animals he was working with choices when asking them questions, and looking for their repeated answers. It's those repeated answers, Duncan suggests, that show us what animals want from us.

The renowned scientist spent many years working on his theory before going public with his thesis. And it's not the first time our very own Dr. Doolittle has made Canadian headlines regarding animal welfare. The changes made in this country's livestock industry, especially to regulations for intensive, or battery, farms for pigs and hens, are a result of Duncan's work.

Friendly Giant

There wasn't anything all that out of the ordinary when Edouard Beaupre was born on July 9, 1881, in the new parish of Willow Bunch, Saskatchewan. He was the firstborn of Gaspard and Florestine Beaupre, who went on to have 19 more children; he was an average size, between 4 and 6 kilograms, and had a normal growth pattern right up until he was three years old. Then everything changed.

To say Edouard "shot up," as many parents often say of their growing youngsters, was an understatement. By the time he was nine, he was 1.82 metres tall, and he stood more than 2 metres tall just eight years later. Eventually, Edouard earned the moniker "Willow Bunch Giant."

To help support his family, the gentle giant looked for ways to use his stature to his advantage. To that end, he became a "strongman" and joined a variety of travelling shows, eventually landing a gig with the Barnum and Bailey Circus. Despite the natural strength that accompanied his size, fighting didn't suit the soft-hearted Edouard, so he used his strength in other ways, such as lifting horses that weighed as much as 410 kilograms over his head, or bending iron bars with his bare hands.

Tragically, Edouard died in St. Louis, where he was performing in the St. Louis World's Fair in 1904, at the tender age of 23, after a two-year battle with tuberculosis. Doctors in attendance recorded his height at 2.51 metres and his weight at 180 kilograms. They also determined that at the time of his death, Edouard was still growing.

Edouard's grief-stricken family was unable to pay the costs of transporting his body back to Willow Bunch. The circus Edouard was working with at the time also refused to pay those costs, so the company that embalmed the young man's body decided to recoup their expenses by putting it on display. Edouard drew in crowds, even after his death.

In an unbelievable show of disrespect, Edouard's body continued to make appearances in museums and circuses until 1907, when the young man's preserved remains made their way to the Université de Montréal. Scientists at the university attributed Edouard's giant status to an abnormally large amount of growth hormone produced and secreted throughout his body by his pituitary gland. After considerable wrangling on Edouard's family's part, he was finally cremated and put to rest on the grounds of the Willow Bunch museum on July 7, 1990.

As Nature Would Have It

Another Canadian claim to fame as far as very tall men goes came to us by way of the British Isles. Angus Mòr MacAskill was born on the Isle of Berneray, Scotland, in 1825, and emigrated with his family to Englishtown on Cape Breton Island about six years later. He reached a height of 2.36 metres in his lifetime, and like others of his stature at that time, MacAskill worked the circus scene and was exhibited alongside the smallest humans of his day. He also demonstrated his profound strength with the usual tricks.

However, what separates MacAskill from other giants over the years was that, as the 1981 edition of the *Guinness Book of World Records* states, he was the world's tallest "true giant," meaning that MacAskill's stature wasn't the result of any abnormality—he was just naturally tall. And with a chest circumference of 200 centimetres, he also boasted the "largest chest measurements of any non-obese man."

DID YOU KNOW?

Toronto native Jerry Sokoloski is currently considered the tallest man in Canada. Measuring 2.24 metres, Sokoloski is a natural at basketball and once considered a career with the NBA. These days you might catch a peek at our nation's tall man in television commercials for Mr. Clean and Bud Light.

A Crazy Kind of Love

I've known people who live, breathe and sleep hockey. Others are immersed in the arts. Still others appear to be addicted to education. But despite the fact that I know of a great many people who enjoy going to the gym several times a day, everyday, I can't say I know a single person who shares this man's passion.

Alberta-born Doug Pruden is a gym junky—no bones about it. He's played team or individual sports for most of his life.

But where this athlete really excels is in doing push-ups. He just loves push-ups; they are his favourite exercise. Pair his love for push-ups with his motivation to better himself with every personal challenge, and Pruden has earned himself international recognition. He's broken so many records that he's even managed to break a few of his own. And to keep things interesting, he has mastered more than the traditional push-up—he's also blown the lid off records using one arm, the back of his hand, as well as fist or knuckle push-ups.

Breaking these records is a mind-boggling feat you'll appreciate all the more if you put yourself through a timed challenge of your own. Here are just a few of his triumphs you can chew over:

- The most "regular" push-ups Pruden has ever done over an eight-hour period was 10,000

- On July 8, 2005, he pummelled the former back-of-hand push-up record with 1781 completed in an hour and earned a spot in that year's *Guinness World Records* book. The previous record holder was Kevin Jetterson, with a 2003 record of 1582 back-of-hand push-ups.

- His one-minute, one-arm record was set in March 2003 after he completed 114 push-ups

- Pruden estimates he's done more than 10.5 million push-ups over his lifetime

- His many records have earned him a place in the Record Holders Republic Hall of Fame in the UK.

We Become What We Think About

When asked what propelled him to the international success he eventually became, Peter Pocklington credited motivational speaker Earl Nightingale. Pocklington listened to

Nightingale's recording, "The Strangest Secret," many times. In it, listeners are challenged with Nightingale's trademark statement, "You become what you think about." (The message is reminiscent of the more recent *The Secret* of self-help fame.)

Adopting that positive outlook certainly got Pocklington off to a great start as far as business goes, and by the age of 25 he was the youngest Ford dealer in Canada with a car dealership of his own to manage. From there, Pocklington extended his interests to include the ownership of several sporting franchises. His acquisition of the Edmonton Oilers in 1976, back when it was still part of the World Hockey Association (WHA), earned him the moniker Peter Puck. But his business acumen didn't end there. He expanded into the food industry, which included dairy, canola and meat-packing ventures, as well as prepared foods. He also branched into real estate and the world of finance. At the height of his empire, Pocklington was pulling in more than $2 billion in sales. And to show goodwill to his fellow Canadians, Pocklington shared a good portion of his wealth, including a $1.5 million donation to the Canadian Cystic Fibrosis Foundation and $2 million to the non-profit youth organization Junior Achievement.

All in all, Pocklington seemed like a great guy, except, of course, when he traded Gretzky. That wasn't cool at all.

In 1998, Pocklington and his wife moved to the U.S., settling into a luxury gated community in Indian Wells, California. It seemed that life was indeed good, and Pocklington was reaping the rewards he'd envisioned. Unfortunately, nothing good lasts forever, no matter how well you visualize it. Some of Pocklington's business interests had suffered over the years for various reasons, and he found himself facing a series of lawsuits.

After struggling for years with the fallout from those lawsuits, Pocklington decided to throw in the towel and declare bankruptcy. Unfortunately, he didn't come clean in bankruptcy court and was sentenced to probation and house arrest when he pleaded guilty to perjury in 2010. Three years later he was in court again facing a six-month jail term for breaching that probation. He appealed the conviction in December 2013, and as of the writing of this book, was still waiting his next court date.

At this point in the complex story of Peter Pocklington, the cliché "the puck stops here" seems appropriate, but we will have to wait to discover where "here" is.

Media Mogul

Some of us work hard to make our way through life, whereas others, like media mogul Conrad Black, get a lucky little boost to get them going. Born in Montréal to a family of means, Black was afforded the best in educational opportunities. His success at those opportunities, however, was questionable at best. At various times during his education Black quit in the middle of a program, failed final exams or was expelled for his behaviour. It's not that Black wasn't smart. He was just incorrigible. Still, he somehow managed to complete a law degree at Université Laval, followed by a Master of Arts degree from McGill University.

Black's business acumen was considerably more impressive than his academic performance, largely because, one might suggest, he had a finger in a lot of pies. He is perhaps best known for his connection to the newspaper industry, and in particular the Canadian-based media company he created, Hollinger Inc. Ironically, Black made his own headlines when he faced fraud convictions, which included "diverting funds for personal benefit," in Chicago's U.S. District Court in 2007. He was sentenced to six and a half years in a federal prison, ordered to repay money to Hollinger and to pay fines of $125,000.

Of course a guilty verdict and sentencing are never the end of the story, especially for the rich and infamous. Black appealed the decision, only to find himself sentenced to another 13 months in jail in September 2011. He was released eight months later, but that didn't spell the end of Black's legal problems. Fines continued to pile up from past judgments, none of which Black ever admitted to. In fact, not only does Black maintain his innocence on all counts, he compared the judicial system in the United States to that of North Korea.

Black faced legal challenges in Canada, too, and the man who once held the position of Officer of the Order of Canada (1990) and an appointment to the Queen's Privy Council for Canada was stripped of those honours. Black is one of just six Officers of the Order of Canada to be stripped of the title.

From Night Danger to Straw House

Artists are known for their eccentric natures, and Canadian Indi folk musician Cud Eastbound is certainly no exception. The banjo-plucking, guitar-playing Eastbound is known for marching to the beat of his own drum, despite years of working as a backup musician and singer. Since 2007, Eastbound has worked on developing his own unique sound that, according to his bio, "crosses lines between classic folk styling, indie rock energy and the passion and intensity often reserved to punk genres." But recently it's Eastbound's living arrangements that are making headlines. In the summer of 2014, after several years of living in PEI and later,

Nova Scotia, Eastbound decided to equip his 1977 Dodge camper van with everything he needed and make his way northwest, to Dawson City, Yukon.

Of course it comes as no surprise to anyone familiar with the Canadian north that a Dodge camper van wouldn't do as a winter residence. It's also no surprise to anyone who knows Eastbound personally to learn he had a solution to that problem. Why not surround his camper van with straw bales? Made perfect sense to Eastbound. One hundred and seventeen bales later his Dodge home was toasty warm.

"I wanted a solution that was temporary and, once I'm done, I can recycle the material in the spring," Eastbound told the CBC, describing the end result as something that looks like a "giant Lego block house made of straw."

Come spring the bales will be recycled and Eastbound will start on plans for his next winter home—one that will be made of wood. And if all goes well for Eastbound in the Yukon, he might even consider changing his name to Northwestbound.

THIS JUST IN: UNIQUE NEWS STORIES

YOU'VE GOT TO BE KIDDING!

We relish the news of our heroes, forgetting that we are extraordinary to somebody too.

–Helen Hayes

As the old cliché goes, there's nothing stranger than the truth. The real world is a goldmine for fiction writers, and on any given day something jaw-dropping happens. Strange but true events also provide this country's news writers with fodder for bizarre headlines—and bizarre headlines sell papers! Just ask gossip rags like HELLO! Canada *and* OK! Magazine.

Odd Coincidence

If you've spent much time driving through British Columbia, you'll probably agree that this news item, strange though it may be, isn't all that surprising. For the rest of you, consider this fair warning of road conditions in that neck of the woods.

Back in May 2010, 49-year-old Kitimat resident Yvonne Studley hit a moose while driving. Hitting a moose is like hitting a granite wall. Studley was seriously injured and was taken to Vancouver General Hospital for treatment. Her sister, 51-year-old Connie Everitt, decided to drive down for a visit. Everitt was driving one car and her husband Steve was leading the way in another. While rounding a corner near 70 Mile House Everitt also struck a moose. Thankfully Everitt's injuries were far less serious than her sister's, but the accident was no slight bump. Had someone been sitting in the passenger seat, they could have been killed from the impact.

THIS JUST IN: UNIQUE NEWS STORIES

Moose Meat Massacre

Greenland sharks are one of the largest sharks in the world, but there are parts of its anatomy that are smaller than one might expect. For example, it has a small head and short snout. And perhaps that's why one of these lovely creatures, which was meandering along to the northeastern shores of Newfoundland, bit off a little more than it could chew—and just about died as a result.

In November 2013, one of these bottom dwellers happened upon a chunk of moose hide, which was likely tossed away by a lucky hunter. Thinking he'd struck pay dirt, the shark started feasting away. There's no telling how long it gnawed on the hide before two locals to Norris Arm North, Derrick Chaulk and Jeremy Ball noticed the poor animal beached and belly up with a furry blob protruding from its mouth. Working together, the men dislodged the roughly 60 centimetres of flesh from the shark's throat and pushed and pulled the creature until they worked it back into deeper water. Not sure if they managed to save the shark, the men stuck around watching from a safe distance. It took about 30 minutes for the shark to regain enough strength to slap its tail and head back to sea.

Chaulk told CBC News that it felt good to see the shark swim away and know that he had a part in saving its life. And I'm sure the shark was doubly happy.

Unwelcome Guests

Garter snakes were quite commonplace for folks living in Poplar Point, Manitoba. It wasn't unusual for me to find a dozen baby snakes sunning themselves along the cracks of the sidewalk between my front step and our family driveway.

Let's just say it's an understatement to suggest I am not a snake lover, but my Poplar Point experience had nothing on that of a Saskatchewan family in the fall of 2014. The Canadian Press reported that as of November 26, the family, who lived in an old farmhouse near Regina, collected a total of 310 plains garter snakes—and they weren't slithering in the grass. Somehow these persistent serpents wiggled their way INSIDE the home.

One would think the inhabitants of this particular farmhouse might be a little unhappy with their visitors, but it appears they took the snakes' presence in stride. And rather than destroying the snakes—which seems like an overwhelming prospect in its own right—they transported them to the Salthaven West Wildlife Rehabilitation & Education Centre. Of that number, 100 were scheduled for transportation to Prince Albert's Saskatchewan Polytechnic campus for further study.

A Batty Situation

If snakes don't make you squeamish, how would you feel about sharing your apartment with bats? Saskatoon resident Christina Abbott first discovered she was sharing her home with a bat on the evening of April 27, 2013. One bat would be annoying, but nothing to leave home over.

However, after having gone away for a week, she returned home to discover more bats in her apartment, and they kept on coming. One day she entered her apartment to find five bats tucked away in assorted locations—one on a window screen, one in an open drawer, and three in the bathtub. Even after the apartment's management tried their hand at getting rid of the creatures, the bats returned, leaving Abbott no choice but to move on to less crowded quarters.

Lone Wolf

According to CBC News, in June 2013 a fisherman named Bob Thacker spotted a strange sight swimming across northern Saskatchewan's Shadd Lake. At first the Vancouver resident thought what he saw was a duck, but the closer he got to the swimmer the more convinced he was that it was something far more unusual—it was a white wolf. Thacker and his fishing guide got close enough to take a short video of the animal, but in a lake the size of Shadd, which stretches 14 kilometres long 5.6 kilometres wide, they didn't want to further stress the swimmer.

CRAZY CRIMES AND OUTLANDISH OUTLAWS

YOU RISKED JAIL FOR THAT?

Crime never makes sense, but after reading the following you'll no doubt agree that some crimes are stranger than others.

Stolen Light Bulbs?

The town of Anyox, BC, sprang up in the early 1900s after large deposits of copper and other precious metals were discovered there. The town was located along Observatory Inlet, about 60 kilometres southwest of Stewart, and was founded by the Granby Mining and Smelting Company around 1912. Within two years, Anyox's population grew to about 3000 people. The town boasted the country's tallest hydroelectric dam and served as a kind of port community, offering ocean vessels a stopping point between Prince Rupert to the north and Vancouver in the south. The town had every amenity residents could ask for, including health professionals, cafés, pool halls and a taxi service. The Masons, Oddfellows and Elks all had a significant presence in the town, which even boasted a golf course. Its future, along with that of the mine that supported it, looked promising. But on January 26, 1940, the *Victoria Times* reported that the town was closed and would soon "be dismantled," making Anyox one of BC's official ghost towns.

Not much remains of the town's heyday, aside from the few artifacts that dot the townsite. Among the more interesting artifacts, found inside the crumbling shell of Powerhouse No. 1, was a collection of light bulbs all bearing the word "Stolen" etched on them.

As it happens, there's a perfectly simple explanation for the word, but it took a little digging to bring it to light.

Istvan Hernadi has led adventure seekers through the Abandoned Towns of Northwest BC, a tour organized by the Continuing Studies Department of the University of Northern British Columbia. In July 2014, Hernadi told Global News that the Granby Consolidated Mining and Smelting Company had an ongoing problem of the theft of light bulbs in their facility—apparently the many benefits of living in Anyox didn't include an adequate supply of bulbs at the local store. And so Granby decided to fight fire with fire, as it were, and have the supplier stamp "STOLEN" in capital letters on each bulb. Anyone brazen enough to use one of these light bulbs in their home clearly admitted to having stolen them.

Apparently the plan didn't have the desired affect. Instead, the light bulbs became a kind of status symbol. According to a 2008 article in *Geoscience Canada,* "some households blatantly displayed the bulbs with the incriminating word while others went to some effort to sand the evidence from the glass."

Bungling Burglar

A Toronto robber made the *Toronto Sun's* weird crime collection in December 2009 after he burrowed his way through drywall and into a hair stylist shop. It was a lot of work just to make off with an estimated $200 and a few cigarettes. He also used the facilities before ditching the joint. But the police were fast on his trail, as it appears the thief left behind his wallet, complete with his identification and parole card.

Mobile Home?

Yukon resident Josie-Anne Pilotte was quite proud of the cabin she constructed with the help of a few friends. It was to be her personal oasis and a chance to own a home of her own. It measured almost 2 metres by 5 metres, and was about 3.5 metres high with an overhang roof, two small windows and a door. It was the perfect size for a wood stove, a bed, maybe a small table and a chair or two. Nothing fancy, just a place to sleep and get away from it all at the end of the day.

The structure was built on a friend's property on Fish Lake Road, just outside of Whitehorse, but Pilotte knew she'd have to move it eventually, and so another friend offered her a site when she was ready to move her house. And when that long-awaited day finally arrived, Pilotte's friends trekked with her to the cabin, only to discover the building had vanished.

"They were prepared," Pilotte said of the thieves in a *Whitehorse Star* article. Any personal contents Pilotte had inside the cabin were discarded nearby, along with any extra materials she hadn't yet used. It appears the culprits dismantled the building, and likely moved it on a flatbed. Pilotte has made several pleas to the public for information on her missing home but has yet to find it.

Surprisingly, Pilotte isn't the only person to lose a house this way. At least one reader of the online version of this story commented that they, too, lost a home to thieves. The reader said thieves made off with a "small, old farm house" he owned—it was removed from a stone foundation, dragged across the lawn and disappeared down the highway. Puts a whole new perspective on the need to lock your doors.

Gone to Pot

BC pot smokers took a hit in 2009 after one of their providers had the RCMP kicking down his door. It all started in January when a White Rock man handed his 11-month-old the house phone to play with. As luck would have it, the toddler dialed 911 then hung up. The call-taker located where the call came from and sent the police. When no one answered their knock, the police kicked in the door, anxious to make sure everyone was okay. Baby and father were fine; so were the 500 marijuana plants police discovered in the process.

Strange Haul

I can think of a lot of stuff criminals would like to steal, but I'm sure you'd agree that a haul of shampoo and mouthwash wouldn't top the list. And yet that's exactly what a pair of thieves took when they broke into the Goderich Drive commercial trucking business in Hamilton, Ontario, in the twilight hours of August 16, 2013. Also stolen were a 2003 blue Freightliner and the 2005 DMND-FV trailer where the products were stashed. According to a CBC article, police couldn't decide if the culprits specifically looked for shampoo and mouthwash to steal, or if it just happened to be the easiest load to grab. The other possibility is the thieves were

Dash for Cash

A 39-year-old Victoria man looking for a quick payday in March 2013 found himself behind bars after a bank teller saw him peering through the bank's windows. A Canadian Press article explained that the teller recognized the man because she'd seen him earlier that same day when he strolled up to her wicket and told her he was "attempting a robbery and wondered if she would give him some feedback on how it was going." When she didn't cough up any dough, the man fled, only to return at the same time as police were taking the teller's statement. The teller noticed the man right away, and police apprehended him shortly thereafter. The man may have denied the accusation, but thanks to the bank's surveillance photos, there was no chance of mistaken identity.

Getting Away with Murder?

My dad always said politicians and lawyers were not to be trusted, but even he never mentioned they could be capable of murder. Yet it appears that back in 1833 one John Wilson of Perth, Ontario, a man who held the positions of lawyer, judge and politician at various times in his life, murdered a man when he was still a law student. The story goes that Wilson and a young Elizabeth Hughes were an item, and another student had the audacity to utter disparaging comments about the maiden's character. Wilson was not one to stand by and have the reputation of the woman he loved besmirched. At that time in Canadian history, settling an argument with a duel wasn't entirely unheard of, and that's exactly what the two men did. After taking the agreed upon number of paces they turned and fired, and the man bold enough to blacken Miss Elizabeth's good name was dead. Wilson fought for his lady's honour, and though he was charged with second-degree murder, he was acquitted and went on to uphold the law for more than three decades.

911, What's Your Emergency?

If you wake up one morning and notice your car isn't where you parked it when you went to bed the night before, calling the police is a good idea, but it's certainly not an emergency. Neither is your neighbour's annoying dog that won't stop barking. Or the graffiti you discovered on your garage. These issues should be directed to your local police station during office hours.

But it appears calling 911 for these kinds of concerns isn't uncommon. In fact, they're troublesome enough that the Internet news site DurhamRegion.com reported local police were giving the public a refresher on when to use the emergency number. The decision to go to the media occurred after an emergency operator was tied up for 10 minutes by a caller complaining that a local grocer "sold him mouldy bread." Initially the man in question returned the bad bread to the grocery store, which in turn replaced it with two more loaves. When the man discovered they too were mouldy, he'd had enough. He called 911.

According to the article as many as 50 percent of all 911 calls are not emergencies. Folks who continue to misuse the service can be charged.

Easy Money?
A 45-year-old Thompson, Manitoba, man found himself in trouble with the law when his employers got suspicious that

something fishy was going on with their security guard. The man collected parking fees at the Thompson airport, but it appears he fudged the details on many of the receipts he turned in and pocketed a cool $12,000 between 2008 and 2010. Although the former guard admitted to the theft, his lawyer pleaded for a conditional discharge hoping to spare him a criminal record, which would mean he'd lose his new job with Thompson's sheriff's office. To make matters worse, the man's wife was Thompson's head sheriff at the time. The judge wasn't concerned with the man's job woes, and she sentenced him to six months house arrest.

My Keys, Please?

I can understand why someone wouldn't have worried about locking his or her car doors back in 1955. I can even understand leaving it running for a short time, especially during some of this country's crazy cold winters. But leaving the doors unlocked and keys in the ignition all the time is just asking for trouble, wouldn't you agree?

Police at the time certainly thought so. In fact, they considered the practice an unnecessary draw on their limited work force when someone's car was actually stolen. So to limit potential thefts and curb the residents' nasty key-in-ignition habit, officers confiscated any keys they noticed left in vehicles. Car owners had to visit their local constabulary and "apply" to get their keys.

LEGISLATION OVERBOARD

YOU MEAN THERE'S A LAW FOR THAT?

Laws are like sausages, it is better not to see them being made.

–Otto von Bismarck

Remember when you were a kid and thought school rules were dumb and parents were perpetually unfair? Try as you might you just couldn't make sense of the steady stream of statues seemingly issued on a daily basis.

As it happens, parents and teachers aren't the only ones you might accuse of instituting odd ordinances. Lawmen in communities around this country have struggled with establishing law and order since the first settlers arrived in this country. It might sound like a simple thing to do, but I challenge you to attend a few of your local town council meetings to see how difficult it actually is to keep voters happy. And as you'll see, there have been a lot of weird rules established over the years that when they were passed may have sounded like a good idea, but in retrospect were, well, strange.

One for the Law Books

This weird law put Prince Edward Island in the news as the only place in North America to officially ban canned pop. The "can ban" as it was known, made it illegal for stores to sell canned pop. It was passed in 1984 for two main reasons: to protect the environment and to provide job security for workers at a local Pepsi bottling plant. (In case you were wondering, plastic bottles were also banned.)

It appears that many Islanders weren't overly enamoured with the law and routinely transported trunk-loads of canned pop with them every time they returned from a trip to the mainland. They were so unhappy with the legislation that in 2007 the issue became a campaign platform, and in May 2008 the ban was finally lifted. After more than two decades of arguing for the ban on environmental grounds, PEI's provincial government now touted the benefits of aluminum.

Hail to the power of the vote…I guess!

Smokin' Hot Debate

Canadians aren't all a bunch of pot-smoking, free loving, hippie Liberals. Still, we might find that label a bit hard to refute in the wake of numerous attempts in recent years by various individuals to push for the legalization of marijuana.

Officials with the Centre for Addiction and Mental Health (CAMH) in Toronto argued in favour of legalization as recently as October 2014. According to a CBC report,

Dr. Jurgen Rehm, director of social and epidemiological research at CAMH argued that regulating the sale of cannabis would mean concerns like potency and purity, for example, would be monitored.

Of course the idea of decriminalization isn't about condoning pot smoking. Rather, it moves the emphasis on the drug from a legal concern to one of harm reduction. It's about reallocating funds from the judicial system to health care, with the goal of ultimately reducing drug abuse.

Liberal Leader Justin Trudeau has certainly been vocal on his stance to legalize weed, echoing medical officials who suggest doing so gives the authorities "more opportunity to keep the drug from children." Of course, legalizing pot would also mean that Trudeau didn't break the law the "at least one time" he admitted to smoking pot since becoming an MP.

Don't Shoot!!

To date, no one has ever found him or herself face to face with a sasquatch—or at least no one has lived to tell the tale. And I don't know about you, but should I ever find myself in such a predicament, gun in hand, I'd be hard-pressed not to use it. It's not that I'm a violent sort of person. It's just that, well, sasquatches are big—or at least that's what we've been told. Remember, no one has clearly seen one of these hairy bipedal creatures.

The question of whether the sasquatch is fact or legend aside, apparently the province of British Columbia at one time had a law stating it was illegal to kill a sasquatch.

LEGISLATION OVERBOARD

Underwater Mischief

It's been suggested that vandalism costs every Canadian upwards of $100 each year. Along with the typical stone through window or car hood smashed, vandals can get pretty creative. Just take a look at the spontaneous works of art that occasionally appear on buildings or railway cars. Still, it's hard to imagine what prompted this strange entry from the pages of Newfoundland's history. The Newfoundland Act of 1892 made it illegal for anyone to break or damage submarine telegraph cable. Now exactly why anyone would go to the trouble of deep sea diving only to hack away at a bunch of iron wires is unclear, but should the diehard vandal choose to do so, the action would cost him $500 or land him in the clink for three months.

Mind Your Business

Pets wandering onto a stranger's property have been an annoyance in most communities at one time or another. But back in 1898, the government of North-West Territories, which stretched from Neepawa, Manitoba, across most of western Canada to the Rocky Mountains, was quite firm on the matter. There were more important squabbles to tend to than a pup relieving itself on a neighbour's lawn. In fact, unless a "lawful fence" adequately protected the offended party from the wandering animal at the time of the crime, officials really didn't have any sympathy for them.

You Can't Wear That!

According to the Encyclopedia Britannica, sociologists and other folks who study modern culture have described Québec as a "post-1960s phenomenon resulting from the Quiet Revolution, an essentially homogenous socially liberal counter-culture...." It's the kind of place I'd think Michael Stivic of *Archie Bunker* fame would approve of. So it's odd that as recently as 1985 the powers that be in the town of D'Outremont enacted a bylaw making it illegal to wear a bathing suit in public. No more sunning yourself at a public park wearing swim trunks or bikinis in that town.

The new law ignited the ire of at least one gent who, as it happened, had been taking his daily jog in his swim trunks and sunning with his sweetie in public parks for some time. He was so disenchanted with the legislation that he stepped up and challenged the municipality. He argued the law denied him rights otherwise guaranteed by the Canadian Charter of Rights and Freedoms. And he won his case, too, ensuring other joggers and sunbathers in D'Outremont can continue to don bathing gear in public to their hearts' content.

In the Nude, You Say?

If the folks in D'Outremont had their concerns about wearing swimsuits in public, I wonder what they would have thought about the swimming bylaws in the towns of Edson, Alberta, and Summerside, PEI?

To begin, let's start at the easternmost city and turn the clock back to the early days of the 20th century. Back then it was perfectly legal to swim in the nude, as long as you did so between the hours of 8:30 pm and 7:00 am.

The folks in Edson enjoyed a similar freedom according to a 1912 bylaw, though their safe naked public bathing times were between 9:00 pm and 6:00 am. Furthermore, it's unclear if it was a misprint in the bylaw, or just a quirk of that community, but any kind of swimming and bathing was restricted to those hours.

Up in Smoke?

There was a time when smoking was thought to be good for your health. In fact, if you visit Sun Drug Store and Bill's Confectionary, located on 1920 Street in Fort Edmonton Park, the "clerk" on duty will echo sentiments from that era and sing you praises about how smoking can cure seasonal asthma.

That said, not everyone was interested in promoting smoking. In fact, the town of Ponoka, Alberta, passed a bylaw in 1914 forbidding anyone from walking into a barn while puffing on a pipe or cigarette. This bit of legislation was no doubt motivated more by the desire to prevent fires than concern about the tar accumulating in the smoker's lungs. Regardless, if you were caught in the act you could find yourself behind bars for up to 30 days or paying a $25 fine. This bylaw was in place until 1998, when it was repealed.

Snowmobiler's Delight

Beausejour is a nice little town with its share of quaint features. But it certainly wouldn't win any awards for drawing large crowds of tourists, especially in winter, even with some of the best burger joints Manitoba has to offer. However, if you and your snowmobile ever find yourself passing through between October 15 and April 15 in any given year, there's one thing Beausejour has to offer—roads for your ride. During those six months snowmobilers can legally share the roads with other vehicles, as long as they adhere to the same rules. The only exception to this privilege is that snowmobiles must stay off Park Avenue and First Street North, the two main streets that connect the town with the main highways.

Shhhh...Not So Loud

Making merry as the clock ticks away and a New Year dawns often means noshing it up big time and partaking of a few too many libations. But the folks down in Williams Lake have a cure for that. It's called a day off. While the rest of the country's population is dragging his or her weary bones back to work, headache and all, Williams Lake residents are nursing their hangovers from the comfort of home.

The idea for the January 2 holiday originated back in the 1930s when a couple of businessmen were sitting in their empty stores, bored silly with nary a customer between them. They got to thinking that maybe it would be a better use of their time to close up shop and stay home like the rest of the town seemed to be doing. The day off started as an unofficial tradition that, in 1943, turned into a holiday. Still, it didn't hit the law books until 1959, when it received the name Wrestling Day because "half the town was wrestling with a hangover." The holiday was challenged in 1976, but residents weren't impressed. They put enough pressure on council that Wrestling Day was reinstated in 1977.

DID YOU KNOW?

It's against the law to name your business, "Parliament Hill," or to use the term to describe any service or product you have for sale.

Nothing is Free

Have you ever stopped to wonder why when you sign a free ticket for a draw, you have to answer a skill-testing question before handing it in? Well, wonder no longer! Sources searching out some of Canada's weird laws have suggested that our federal government has a problem with someone getting something for nothing. And so if you want to win that case of beer or shiny barbecue, you'd better do your due diligence and answer the question.

LEGISLATION OVERBOARD

WHERE THERE'S A WILL, THERE'S A WAY

Special Distinction

Canadians are the best hosts; we really will give you the shirt off our backs if necessary. But in 1943, the Canadian government's hospitality made the history books when Ottawa's Civic Hospital welcomed the first royal baby ever to be born in North America. Baby Margriet Francisca made her grand entry on January 19, 1943. Her mother, Dutch Crown Princess Juliana, and her family had been exiled and were living in Canada, where they stayed from June 1940 until June 1945.

By all accounts Princess Juliana enjoyed an active social life while living in Ottawa, but birthing a baby on foreign soil presented her with a tricky problem—that baby wouldn't have full Dutch citizenship. To rectify that situation the maternity suite where Margriet was born was designated "extraterritorial" by the Canadian government, ensuring the newborn would indeed have the full Dutch citizenship she required to keep her title as princess. In gratitude for this action, and for the sacrifice made by Canadian soldiers in the Netherlands during its Nazi invasion, Princess Juliana gifted the Canadian government in Ottawa with 100,000 tulip bulbs—the first in a series of tulip bulb gifts sent by the Dutch government each year. It was this kindness that led to Ottawa's annual Canadian Tulip Festival.

LEGISLATION OVERBOARD

Buyer Beware?

There's been a suggestion floating around on the Internet that Canadians can claim dog food as a tax deduction. If that were true it would certainly be weird.

Sorry to burst your bubble folks, but it's false—at least for the most part. As with every rule, and as strange as it may seem, there are exceptions. For example, if you have an assistance dog for medical reasons you might be able to claim expenses for the dog's care, including its food, on your income taxes. But one story even out-weirds that little loophole. According to the well-known income tax authority H&R Block, there was at least one case where a farmer claimed cat and dog food because "they were outdoor pets meant to keep wildlife away from their blueberries."

Seriously!

CANADIAN INGENUITY AT ITS FINEST

The invention of basketball was not an accident. It was developed to meet a need. Those boys simply would not play "Drop the Handkerchief."

–James Naismith

Canadians aren't known for boasting, but when it comes to innovation Canada has a lot to brag about. Among our most popular inventions are life-saving insulin, the comic hero Superman, and, of course, the game of basketball. What follows are some of the stranger inventions we are also credited with.

A Spa with a Twist

One doesn't normally think of cold as comforting, but Vernon's Sparkling Hill's Cryotherapy Cold Sauna has no shortage of customers. As the only cold sauna on the continent, this specialty spa features temperatures that dip as low as −110°C. The treatment promises some relief from pain caused by inflammation, such as the kind experienced by athletes. It costs about $300 for 10 three-minute treatments, and repeated treatments are necessary for the best results. But if you do decide to try this unique healing method, don't even think of stretching an individual visit beyond the three-minute mark. Sneak in a few more minutes and it could be the last cryotherapy treatment—or any treatment—you'll ever receive.

Bark Art

You really have to see this to believe it. Paper-thin birch bark folded and held by nimble fingers that feed the bark through teeth, a little like a seamstress feeding material through the grips of a sewing machine. To the observer, the end result looks like nothing more than a series of cuts on a wad of bark. But when that sheet of bark is unfolded a mini-masterpiece is revealed!

The art of birch bark biting was practiced by the Ojibwa, Cree and Algonquian First Nations peoples. These bitings were sometimes completed during friendly competitions, and at other times the resulting print would be used as a pattern for bead or porcupine appliqué work. Manitoba Cree artist Angelique Merasty (1924–96) pushed the envelope a lot further by turning the Native craft into a fine art with her detailed images of flowers, insects, animal and humans.

Frightening Alternative

This contribution to strange Canadian stories isn't an easy one to categorize, but many of you reading this will certainly have heard of its originator. John George Diefenbaker was the 13th Prime Minister of this great country; he governed from 1957 to 1963—a time when the development of nuclear weapons was on the rise. It must have made him a bit nervous because he is credited with building a top-secret nuclear missile shelter, sometime between 1959 and 1961, equipped with many amenities. The Diefenbunker, as it's now called, is a huge underground bunker measuring just over 30 square kilometres and designed to protect Canada's government elite should a nuclear attack occur. Today, the site is part of Canada's Cold War Museum and has been part of several public events, including *The Amazing Race Canada*.

Technological Marvel

Dragonfly Innovations, a Saskatoon-based company, made Canadian aviation history in November 2014 when a drone designed and produced by the company was added to the Smithsonian Air and Space Museum.

The idea for drones, likely named for the humming sound they make while flying, has been around since the mid-1800s, with actual prototypes being developed as early as the beginning of the 1900s. In case you were wondering, as I was when I first heard this story, a drone is small unmanned aerial vehicle (UAV) often used by the military and law enforcement. Dragonfly Innovations is recognized for leading the way in drone technology because they were smart enough to recognize there was a real, practical use for the technology. It was one of their creations that helped the RCMP track down a missing man who'd wandered away from a car accident, saving them precious time in getting him the help he needed.

Of course the possibility of these drones being used for less altruistic purposes can lead to privacy issues—the idea of having your neighbour peeking through your window at will is disconcerting. So Transport Canada established a set of regulations limiting a person's ability to use UAVs, especially when in the vicinity of people and animals, as well as buildings, structures or vehicles.

A Draining Proposition?

This story is about taking video gaming—and blood donations—to the extreme.

Avid gamers and long-time friends Taran Chadha and Jamie Umpherson developed the idea of tying real-life blood donations to the playing of a video game in an effort to boost blood donations in Canada. That said, I'm sure a decent profit margin for the creators was another consideration.

In any case, according to Blood Sport's creators, the way the game works is "stupidly simple." When a player is shot during the game, a signal is sent to the controller and turns on a blood collection system that is, of course, intravenously attached to that player's arm.

"We are simply creating the gaming hardware that will allow us to get gamers thinking about more important issues while still doing what they love.... From there, we'll partner with the appropriate organizations in both the gaming and medical communities to bring it all to life," Chandha and Umperson are quoted in a written explanation in Yahoo's Daily Buzz.

The pair pitched their idea on Kickstarter, an organization that offers creators of all genres a platform to pitch their ideas, garner public interest and raise the funds necessary to bring their projects from the planning stage to fruition. But when Blood Sport was just $3300 into its $250,000 quest for funds, Kickstarter shut it down. Not to be discouraged, at the writing of this book Chandha and Umperson were still planning to approach blood-donation organizations with their idea.

Unfortunate Claim to Fame

Alexis St. Martin was simply a Canadian fur trader working at a trading post on Mackinac Island, a small island resort located on the American side of Lake Huron, when a freak accident changed the course of his life...and the course of medical history. Details aren't clear, but reports indicate that on June 6, 1822, St. Martin was shot in his side at close range with a musket. It was a through-and-through shot that left a gaping hole in the man's stomach.

To say it was shocking that St. Martin survived is an understatement, and he likely wouldn't have had it not been for a U.S. army surgeon named William Beaumont, who was stationed nearby. Beaumont treated St. Martin's wound, and for the first 17 days monitored St. Martin's progress. During that time, Beaumont noticed that he could watch the food his patient ate re-emerge and escape through the fistula, an abnormal, permanent opening created by the wound. Eventually St. Martin's wounds healed—all but the opening. The hole in his stomach, which eventually shrank from the size of a fist to the size of a loonie, remained.

With the unfortunate Canadian trapper and his injuries, Beaumont, a doctor of limited education and experience, knew he had the chance of his career. And before long, for the first time in recorded history, a study of the process of human digestion was underway. In fact, Beaumont allegedly went so far as to have the illiterate St. Martin sign a contract agreeing to his becoming Beaumont's servant, and he used the man as a human guinea pig of sorts for several experiments. The doctor then wrote extensively about his observations in his 1838 book *Experiments and Observations on the Gastric Juice, and the Physiology of Digestion*.

What Beaumont's investigation did for the medical community was to answer the question of whether human digestion was chemical or mechanical. Beaumont's experiments determined that digestion was indeed a chemical process caused by gastric juices, which were mostly made up of hydrochloric acid, and his work in the field gave him notoriety among his colleagues. That said, were it not for the accident that caused St. Martin considerable discomfort, the questions surrounding human digestion may have remained unknown for some time.

And so let it go down in the annals of Canadian human history that Alexis St. Martin, an otherwise unknown fur trapper hailing from Québec, provided the vehicle by which medical history was made.

STRANGE BUT TRUE UNIQUE CANADIAN CONTRIBUTIONS

CHEERS TO CANADIAN CULINARY CREATIONS

Lassoing a Different Kind of Wild

Newfoundland is known for once housing one of the busiest airports in the world, being one part of the province of Newfoundland and Labrador, having its own time zone and being the first place in North America where European explorers—namely the Vikings—landed. And now The Rock—as it is fondly known—is rapidly gaining another kind of international notoriety for its contributions to the vodka industry.

Since 1995, the Canadian Iceberg Vodka Corporation has been lassoing icebergs off the coast of Newfoundland to produce their product, making the aptly named Iceberg Vodka the only one in the world made from the naturally pure water of icebergs. The reason for harvesting icebergs is simple: they provide the company with the purest water source, and any contaminants they might contain are virtually undetectable.

The icebergs are harvested in spring and are hauled from Iceberg Alley directly to the processing plant in St. John's. Add a little thrice-distilled sweet corn from Ontario and, voilà, you have the world-famous Iceberg Vodka.

Canadian Confections

The Dutch have their Oliebollen, and the Americans have their Krispy Kremes, but we Canadians…we have our beaver tails. The "deliciously addictive whole-wheat pastry," as the official Beaver Tails website describes it, is shaped to look like a beaver's tail and can be ordered with all kinds of toppings, from butter and cinnamon sugar to bananas and chocolate. The idea for the uniquely Canadian pastry started back in 1978 when Killaloe, Ontario, residents Grant and Pam Hooker decided to test their fortunes in the business world by baking and selling their family's traditional fried dough concoction. Within two years of their first sales at a local community fair, the couple opened their first Beaver Tails stand, and today the humble venture has extended into franchise territory, with almost three dozen retail stores operating internationally, including South Korea and Japan.

DID YOU KNOW?

U.S. President Barack Obama enjoys Beaver Tails so much that he stopped by Ottawa's ByWard Market to buy one on his way to the airport after a visit to the Canadian capital, on February 19, 2009. In his honour, the company created a variation called the "Obama Tail."

Bags or Bottles?

If you're like me and prefer to purchase your milk in bags in order to limit the amount of plastic waste filling recycle depots, you might not realize that bagged milk isn't available everywhere. Milk can be purchased this way in select locations in Manitoba and Ontario.

Of course there are some of you who might have never heard of buying milk in bags in the first place. So to enlighten you, let me explain. Milk sold this way usually comes in three single bags wrapped in one large bag and sold as a 4-litre pack. And because filling a glass straight from the bag might prove a bit tricky, you can purchase a reusable pitcher to put your bag in for an easy pour, along with clips to seal the unused portion.

Spicy Surprise

You may not be surprised to learn that our country's agriculture and agri-food system generated $103 billion in 2012 alone, but I'll bet most Canadians don't know that that we are the world's largest exporter, and the second largest producer, of mustard! According to the Canadian Special Crops Association, mustard seed exports averaged $70 million between 2002 and 2007. That represents between 75 and 80 percent of all global mustard exports and translates to 140,000 to 300,000 tonnes of mustard seed each year. Apparently several varieties of the mustard plant really like our climate.

Hot dogs, anyone?

STRANGE BUT TRUE UNIQUE CANADIAN CONTRIBUTIONS

Fire Water

Folks from The Rock have contributed salt pork, salt beef and scrunchins (deep fried pork skin) to the Canadian diet. It might not sound too appetizing, but many argue it's an easily acquired taste. Still, it's likely Newfoundlanders' love of screech, their own version of the 40-proof rum originally shipped from Jamaica and the West Indies in exchange for salt fish that they're most famous for. Legend has it that the rum got its name during World War II after an American serviceman visiting Newfoundland tossed back a shot and got quite a shock. His cries of discomfort were so loud and disturbing that bystanders rushed to his side to help, only to be calmed by the bartender who told them the "screech" they heard was because of the rum the serviceman downed. And so the name—and the Screech tradition—was born. Yowser!

Only In Canada, Eh?

Did you know that ketchup potato chips are uniquely Canadian? They were created here and apparently can't be purchased anywhere outside of our home and native land.

SOMETHING FOR EVERYONE

MEMBERS ONLY

Not everyone can afford a membership to Disney's Club 33 or has the IQ to land a spot in the Giga Society—there are only six members in this international club and each has an IQ of 195 or higher—but that doesn't really matter. As the song goes, sometimes you just want to go where everybody knows your name.

It just so happens that there is no shortage of Canadian clubs—and I don't mean the whisky—for every quirky preference a person might have. And most of them don't require a huge entry fee, or a high IQ. In fact, some of them just encourage you to pony up to the bar! Really! We Canadians are so easygoing.

Sourtoes Anyone?

You may have heard of kissing the cod down east and the recognition the tradition earns you in various Atlantic communities, but you may not have heard about a similar, albeit newer, tradition in Dawson City, Yukon. According to one website, to earn your stripes in this city you must first visit an establishment called the Sourdough Saloon (a "sourdough" is someone who's survived at least one Yukon winter) and ask for a local character known as Captain River RatStep (perhaps alluding to Captain. Dick Stevenson, former riverboat captain and the guy who allegedly came up this tradition).

If you're thinking this sounds weird already, just wait. It gets better. When you meet Captain River RatStep you'll need to ask for at least one ounce of your favourite libation, preferably Yukon Jack. (Originally you had to chug a beer glass full of champagne.) You'll then need to pledge the "Sourtoe Oath" and down your drink—but not before old RatStep drops a dehydrated toe inside. Of course, drinking the drink isn't all you're expected to do. As the saying goes, "You can drink it fast, you can drink it slow, but your lips have gotta touch the toe." That done, you're a member of the prestigious Sourtoe Cocktail Club!

The club was established in 1973, but its roots date back to the 1920s and a pair of rumrunner brothers named Louie and Otto Linken. Apparently as the brothers were conducting one of their cross-border business deals, with the Mounties close on their heels, they came upon poor winter weather. In their rush, Louis accidentally soaked his foot in icy water and didn't take the time to dry off it. Unfortunately, his big toe froze solid. Concerned that potentially life-threatening gangrene could set in, Otto anesthetized his brother with their highly concentrated booze and chopped off Louie's toe. They preserved the toe in...what else?...alcohol.

So exactly how did the toe make its way into someone's drink? According to the legend, Captain Dick Stevenson discovered the toe some years later in an abandoned cabin, and he and a couple of his buddies came up with the idea for the Sourtoe club. Today, the club has more than 100,000 members.

Hold the Toe!

The toe you might pucker up to should you decide to join the Sourtoe Cocktail Club will not be Louie's preserved toe. Oh no. Some patron downed the original toe along with the 100-proof it was floating in. No kidding! Since then, so many folks have swallowed toes that the club has put an official fine in place, and that is NOT a club you want to belong to. The fine for such an offence was $500 just a while back, but it's been jacked up to $2500 today.

The fine hike took place in August 2013 after an American sauntered into the pub, ordered a Sourtoe cocktail, downed it toe and all, and paid the $500 without even being asked. Toe swallowing is so common, in fact, that the saloon routinely collects reserve toes, just in case. Most donated toes are the result of amputations from medical procedures or have been removed post-mortem. But the largest toe donation came from an unnamed miner who had an unfortunate incident with a bulldozer and lost five of his lower digits. On the rare occasion when the pub is completely out of toes, improvisations are made and other body parts are used, including the testicles and penis bone of a black bear.

Appetizing, ain't it?

Not Since Moses Run

This event requires considerably more effort from its participants than simply swallowing their favourite beverage—although that favourite beverage might be the reward they look forward to once they cross the finish line. This dash for glory is called the "Not Since Moses Run" and requires participants to sprint into the Bay of Fundy.

So what exactly is involved, you ask? Adult participants can choose between a 5- or 10-kilometre run that takes them directly into the bay at low tide and has them hustling back to shore before the world-renown high tides overtake them. (I kid you not when I say the highest tides in the world have been recorded here, and they can be unpredictable.) Kids can participate, too, but their event is called The Basket Run, held under the watchful eyes of their parents, and takes place on courses between 100 and 500 metres along the shoreline.

There's a cost to enter the event, and small prizes are awarded. Much of the extra money raised goes to local causes. And although participants aren't part of an official "club" once they've participated, they experience something more life altering. As one participant wrote, "I will carry it in my soul forever."

OMMMMM....

Yoga provides its own kind of high, so imagine what a yoga class on one of the Rockies' highest peaks might do for your mood. It'll cost you more than $500 to jump aboard a helicopter and fly to your outdoor classroom, but according to the website promoting the experience, it's well worth the fee. The class not only offers patrons a tour of some of the Rockies' most spectacular scenery, it offers a combination of "mindful meditation, stretching, balancing and core strengthening" with fresh, crisp mountain air and a picnic lunch. SCORE!

SOMETHING FOR EVERYONE

Making a Splash!

We all know Canadians love their hockey, but I'd bet you didn't know that underwater hockey is also popular in this country? The game, which sees divers chasing a heavy puck along a pool floor to score a goal in their opponent's net, originated in the United Kingdom in 1954.

We Canucks jumped on board in 1962 after Aussie scuba instructor Norm Leibeck introduced the sport to his dive club in Vancouver, BC. Clearly we must have made an impression because the first official international competition, the Underwater Hockey World Championship, was held in Canada in 1980.

But if you think underwater hockey is strange, underwater ice hockey escalates the love of the sport to an altogether outrageous level. In this rendition of Canada's beloved sport, divers don scuba gear to brave the cold and submerge themselves through a hole in the ice. From there the entire game is played upside down with each team chasing a floating puck made of Styrofoam and wood along the ice with the same goal in mind—to score in the other guy's net. At this point Canadians have yet to tackle this sport in any official way. But considering how many polar bear swims take place in this country every January, I'd wager it's only a matter of time before our own national team competes in the Underwater Ice Hockey World Cup.

Full Circle

They're hatched there…and return, between four and six years later, to die. This unique oceanic experience offers patrons more than a chance at the catch of a lifetime, it offers an experience to watch the salmon's final voyage before death. More so, at various times during the course of this unique

wilderness trek, the Campbell River Snorkel Run offers participants a chance to see all five salmon species, by the hundreds of thousands, return to the river from which they were hatched. To do this you'll don a wetsuit to keep you from becoming hypothermic, snorkel and mask so you can see and breathe, and you'll spread your arms and surrender yourself to the current to immerse yourself in another world. It's a life and death journey…one that few get a chance to witness.

A Different Kind of Wild

Any Canadian that has completed Grade 4 Social Studies has no doubt heard of Toronto's CN Tower. At 553.33 metres in height, it was recognized as an architectural wonder when it was completed in 1976 with the distinction of being the "world's tallest free-standing structure [and] tower." And it kept this status until 2007, when Dubai's Burj Khalifa, which when completed in 2010 reached a final height of 829.8 metres, surpassed the CN Tower's height while still under construction. In 1995, the American Society of Civil Engineers named the CN Tower as one of the modern Seven Wonders of the World.

Of course such a structure is bound to attract all kinds of attention. Stuntmen have leapt off the building. World-renown climber and public advocate Dan Goodwin climbed the outside of the building not once, but twice in the same day, rappelling down between climbs. And the CN Tower also provides the public with an unparalleled view of the city and its environs from its observation decks and in-house revolving restaurant.

But in 2011, the building's administration took things a step further when they offered yet another North American—and world—first. This time, they gave the public an opportunity to walk around the perimeter of the roof of the main pod of the tower. To do this and live to tell the tale, participants wear a harness and are attached to an overhead safety system. According to the tower's website, "trained EdgeWalk guides encourage participants to push their personal limits, allowing them to lean back over Toronto with nothing but air and breathtaking views of Lake Ontario beneath them." The entire experience lasts an hour and a half, with the walking portion taking about 30 minutes to complete.

What will we crazy Canucks think of next?

Decision Time
Reality or fiction? You decide.

Apparently a law was passed in London, England, in 1842, suggesting rock-paper-scissors was a perfectly acceptable, legal way to make a decision and was "subject to all relevant contract and tort law." Immediately after the law was issued, the World RPS (as in Rock, Paper, Scissors) Society was formed.

So what, you ask, does an obscure law in Victorian England have to do with crazy Canadiana? Well, it appears that various places in Canada, like Toronto and Winnipeg, have been the site of the World RPS Society Championships. Prizes range from $500 for third place to $1500 and $10,000 for second and first place, respectively. Canadians have been lucky enough to claim many prizes over the years. Seriously.

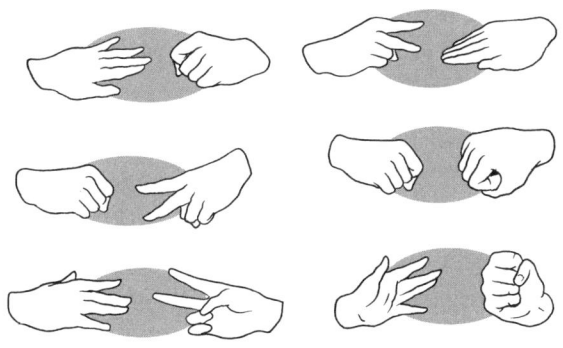

Na-na-na-na-na-na-na-na Batman!

Who says the world of academia is boring? We Canadians certainly know how to spice up our studies with new and innovative approaches. Take the University of Victoria for example. They introduced an exciting new program to their school calendar in 2012—The Science of Batman. The course promised to explore "the extreme range of adaptability of the human body…through the life of the Caped Crusader." No kidding! Batman himself was being used as a metaphor for "the ultimate in human conditioning."

WE CANADIANS KNOW HOW TO PARTY!

BUILDING ON A GREAT IDEA

That's the best revenge of all; happiness. Nothing drives people crazier than seeing someone have a good…life.

–Chuck Palshniuk

Did you know that some scholars believe the first music festivals took place in Ancient Egypt around 4500 BC? As in the festivals of today, there was music and dancing and feasting involved. There was also some kind of religious or political significance to these gatherings— also not unlike today.

Like the Egyptians of old, Canadians love to party. In 2013 the Canadian Encyclopedia reported there were almost "200 major and numerous minor festivals" held in this country annually. Some, like Yellowknife's Long John Jamboree, appeal to a local audience. Others, like the Toronto Garlic Festival, appeal to patrons of a particular culinary bent.

And then there are others.…

Long, Beautiful Hair?

Yellowknife's annual winter festival is called Long John Jamboree. Nothing too strange about that. Their "Growing Challenge," on the other hand, is a tad unusual. As part of their 2014 festival, which was held from March 27 to 29, men were encouraged to grow their facial hair. They were given January 15 as the last day they could shave, and the judging was held on March 28. Points were given for "length, density, appearance and overall bushiness."

Now if you're thinking, "How unfair. What about the women?" Not to worry. Women were also given a chance to shine by growing their leg hair! The same point system applied.

Giant Misfortune

The folks from People for the Ethical Treatment of Animals (PETA) would have been on a rampage worthy of a herd of elephants should this historic oddity have occurred in today's more sensitive era. But back in the day, carting exotic animals about for human entertainment without much thought to their comfort or safety was commonplace. For some, it was especially lucrative.

Such was the case with P.T. Barnum and his famed Barnum and Bailey Circus. P.T. Barnum was a lot of things, both good and questionable, but by his own admission he was a showman first. His goal was to put "money in his own coffers," and the more the better. Sometimes that meant having the best in entertainment for the vast numbers of patrons who crowded into his tents. But it also meant padding his entertainment with whatever he could to ensure something new and unbelievable with every show, including a hoax or two.

Jumbo the African elephant wasn't a hoax; he was the real thing. Back in the 1880s when Barnum was touring him into Canada, Jumbo was the largest elephant ever in captivity. Of course that meant Jumbo, a mammoth creature not typical of North America, was a huge draw when he sauntered up to St. Thomas, Ontario, in 1885. Sadly, Jumbo met with a sudden death on his second visit, September 15, when he came face to face with a Grand Trunk locomotive. It was a tragedy, and one that needed to be dealt with for practical reasons. But how do you inter an elephant?

Some stories suggest that St. Thomas butchers dealt with the carcass, and the elephant meat—not much of a draw for consumers in those days—was burned in a large bonfire that drew the odd person, fork in hand, to test the exotic flesh just so they could say they ate elephant. Taxidermists stuffed the hide, and Jumbo's skeleton was apparently wired together and put on display, making a sad end even sadder.

But 100 years later, long after Barnum himself had died and the circus was sold to the Ringling Brothers, the folks down in St. Thomas decided to recognize the deceased elephant in a big way. The town had a life-sized statue built in his memory. It was constructed in Sussex, New Brunswick, and had to be built in two parts so the pieces could make the 1722 kilometre trip, clearing any bridge structures or narrow roadways along the way. And when it finally arrived at its destination, the 38-ton structure was unveiled on June 28, 1985, followed by a five-day celebration called "Jumbo Days."

Green Goodness

The Festival des Choux de Bruxelles, or Brussels Sprout Festival, celebrates the power food punch of the Brussels sprout. But if you think a festival about the humble sprout is odd, stranger still is how it arrived in the small village of Rogersville, New Brunswick, in the first place. It is a story of serendipity—how one chance connection, a decision to take one road over another, resulted in a local love for Brussels sprouts and the inevitable establishment of a festival to honour the little cabbages.

It's simple really. Brussels sprouts are a staple food in Belgium, and when Trappist monks from that country crossed the Atlantic and established a monastery in Rogersville, they brought their cuisine preferences with them. These monks first planted the mini cabbage heads in Canada in 1905. The sprouts are easy to grow, taste good—if you know how to cook them—and best of all are high in vitamin K, vitamin C, vitamin A and other nutrients. Regular consumption of Brussels sprouts is also said to reduce the risk of developing some forms of cancer. Health benefits aside, though, an old Belgian tradition is to eat the sprouts at the beginning of a meal to avoid getting drunk. Apparently substantial libations are part of most meals in that part of the world.

For all their positive qualities, Brussels sprouts deserve a little kudos—and the folks in Rogersville have paid their respects in a big way with the establishment of the Festival Des Choux de Bruxelles.

Tickle Those Ivories

So, I live just outside of Edmonton and I've never heard of this annual festival. And I couldn't find out much about the society that hosts this event—like when the society was actually founded. But the festival is legit—and it has been hosted annually since at least 2009, if the group's online album is any indication.

The Edmonton Accordion Society meets every second Wednesday, encouraging what many might consider to be a dying art. To further celebrate the "squeeze box," the society hosts its annual EXTRAVAGANZA in August or September. And now that you know about it, if you live in Alberta, consider checking it out!

An Artery-clogging Good Time

We Canadians are proud to claim poutine as our own—it was created in Québec in the late 1950s—and there is even an annual festival to celebrate the cheesy comfort food. The Festival de la Poutine takes place in Drummondville, runs for three days, and serves up a selection of yummy cheese curd and gravy fries, along with a ton of great music.

And if you thought poutine was strictly a Canadian dish, you might be interested to hear that folks south of the border are only too happy to chime in on the festivities. In fact, Chicago has jumped on the bandwagon by hosting a poutine festival of its own. Poutine Fest is, as its website claims, "Chicago's competition of Canada's popular late-night fast food favourite—crispy French fries and cheese curds covered in rich gravy." Now doesn't that sound yummy? Its website also spells romance: "Just think of Poutine Fest as the first of many love letters exchanged between a tipsy, slurring Chicago and picturesque French Canada, somewhere around 3:00 am on a Saturday night…"

So if you find yourself south of the border and hankering for something that reminds you of home, remember this: poutine is available more places than you think. So munch on!

Ice Palaces

People outside of Canada tend to stereotype those of us who live here as having igloos for homes. In some imaginative minds, our walls are made of ice, and snow dominates our landscapes. So the idea of an igloo festival seems apt, if you were speaking with folks from more southern climes.

Talk to someone from Canada and, well, we kind of get our panties in a bunch when someone suggests we all live in igloos. However, this is a big country. There's a lot of space north of '60—that's where it's really cold for those of you who, living in more comfortable climes, may not be aware—and in that part of the country, igloos are still sometimes used for shelter during hunting expeditions. The snow structures have also been used as temporary shelters for generations. So, all things considered, it makes sense that, somewhere in Canada, a community would celebrate the igloo.

Montréal, however, isn't the location that would come to my mind as a host for such an event. And yet, that's exactly where the annual Igloofest is held. Since 2007, the city has hosted the event. Initially the festival ran for three weekends, but it has grown since its inception and now runs for a fourth weekend, drawing as many as 85,000 fans. As part of the winter celebration, every year festival-goers can take part in a "One-Piece" contest—as in who has the best one-piece snowsuit. Prizes for the best winter gear can include everything from winter wear to V.I.P. tickets to the best shows of the season.

Go figure.

Soap Central

It's called Pingfest, and it's been held in parts of Nova Scotia during the Canada Day long weekend since 1996. So far, fans of the long-running English soap opera *Coronation Street,* or 'Corrie' as many fans have chosen to nickname it, have celebrated 50 Pingfests. It's a low-key celebration, focused on the simple things in life and television celebrity. Folks get together to talk about the show, discuss storylines, and enjoy good food and a drink or two. That's it—nothing fancy. It's just a great way to spend a night out.

Kitchens and More

Albertans familiar with this festival understand the Newfie concept of a kitchen party. In short, there's no better time to be had. If you live in Newfoundland and host a kitchen party, everyone you know (and countless folks you don't) will gather in your kitchen to eat and drink, gather 'round a wood stove to strum whatever stringed instruments might be available and kick up one's heels for a night of revelry.

If the kitchen gets too crowded, people spill into the living room, the front yard and anywhere else they can fit.

Sorry to cause any unnecessary mental whiplash, but try to wrap your mind around this. Leap across the country from Newfoundland to Alberta: in particular, the communities of Grande Prairie and Fort McMurray. Many Newfies live in these parts—I know several of them. Lovely people. Know how to party. And I've heard of kitchen parties, although I've never been to one…sadly. But the East Coast Garden Party held in Grand Prairie and Fort Mac opens the door to people like myself so we can have the opportunity to participate in this cultural custom—or at least a rendition of it.

Getting Screeched
If you're not a Newfoundlander, but you'd like to be, this is what you need to do. Grab a whole fish, a thick slice of baloney, the traditional Sou'Wester rain gear, a bottle

of Screech and a list of Newfie words. You'll also need a natural-born Newfoundlander to conduct the complicated ceremony.

As a candidate for Newfie honours, you'll stand by the natural-born Newfoundlander in front of a group of witnesses, where you'll eat the baloney, also known as Newfie steak, kiss the fish and down a full shot of Screech after saluting with the traditional words, "Long may your big jib draw!"

Chocolate Haven

The oldest candy company in Canada is Ganong Brothers of St. Stephen, New Brunswick. Founded in 1873 by brothers James and Gilbert, this company has sweetened the palates of Canadians with a huge variety of treats like cinnamon chocolate chicken bones and, of course, the Pal-o-Mine—a dark chocolate, fudgy, coconut and peanut bar that first ran off the assembly line in 1920. Incidentally, Pal-o-Mine was the first chocolate bar to hit store shelves in an individual wrapper.

Of course, chocolate is king among cravings—and a need, not merely a want, for a large portion of the world's population. And because the province of New Brunswick is responsible for meeting a good portion of that need, it only makes sense that they celebrate the culinary success of their ancestors, not to mention the boost the Ganong Brothers provide to the economy of the Atlantic province. To that end, the first Chocolate Fest was held in 1984 to celebrate the province's chocolate history. Today, this festival is heralded as one of the five best chocolate festivals in the world. Bet you couldn't guess what organizers chose as their official mascot? It's a chocolate brown, furry moose with pink antlers known as "The Great Chocolate Mousse."

WE CANADIANS KNOW HOW TO PARTY!

Bathtub Bonanza?

Motorboats move aside—bathtubs take the lead when it comes to Nanaimo Harbour's annual racing derby.

In 1967, Nanaimo celebrated Canada's 100th birthday by hosting its first ever bathtub race. Every summer since then, as many as 200 racers have jumped aboard "bathtubs" of various designs and competed to see who will be the first to complete the 60-kilometre course from Nanaimo to Vancouver's Fisherman's Cove.

Rusty Harrison of Vancouver, the race's first winner, logged a time of 3:26—today, racing results are broken down into fractions of seconds. The rules for the event have also changed since that inaugural race, but participants are still provided with general instructions on how to construct their own bathtub. Judging by the ongoing popularity of Nanaimo Marine Festival's bathtub races, this is one weird event that will continue to draw the crowds.

A Hairy Good Time

The resort community of Harrison Hot Springs, BC, has drawn crowds to the area since 1886, when it was formally established following the opening of the Canadian Pacific Railway. Initially, folks flocked there for the therapeutic benefits of the hot springs—and, of course, the amazing scenery. But by 1949 the resort had blossomed into an incorporated village where people lived year round. A steady population requires basic amenities, and with the stores, doctors' offices and the like, the folks of Harrison Hot Springs also made sure there's a lot of fun things to do in the area, aside from soaking in the sulphur-laden titular springs, of course.

For example, there's the Bald Eagle Weekend that runs at the end of November. Take in this event and you'll be treated to as many as 10,000 bald eagles feasting on the millions of salmon that return to the area and spawn every fall. Then there's the Festival of Trees, Family Fun Carnival, Tulips of the Valley Festival and Festival of the Arts, along with several activities advertised on a weekly basis in the community's weekly "Fresh Sheet."

But perhaps the most unusual attraction locals promote is the annual Sasquatch Days. The first Sasquatch Days took place on May 23 and 24, 1938, and was a joint event hosted by local government and the Sts'ailes First Nations. It drew 2000 First Nations people from this country and our neighbours to the south. Activities included canoe races, salmon barbecues and medicine walks, but the biggest draw was the sasquatch.

The same holds true for today's festivities. Of course the "wild man" of Sts'ailes legend doesn't actually make an appearance at the annual event. Nonetheless, the creature that inhabits such a place of honour among the local indigenous peoples is still front and centre in the festivities. And local sasquatch investigators and Sts'ailes experts steeped in oral stories passed down through the generations regale festival participants with their knowledge of the elusive creature.

Living the Fantasy

Gone are the days when farmers, especially young people wanting to buy into and make their living on the family farm, could survive solely on their crops and livestock. It's a problem that's given rise to what some call value-added or diversified farming, simply meaning that farmers are increasing their earning power by providing additional goods or services. Some farmers have established onsite markets that include homemade crafts and other goods. Others have hosted unique events, like pumpkin hunts and fall festivals.

Then there are others that have tried an assortment of activities. Such is the case with Chilliwack's Fantasy Farms. They kick the year off with Easter on the Farm, followed by the Chilliwack Corn and Country Music Festival, The Reapers Haunted Attraction and The Maze of Terror, Petey's Pumpkin Patch and Petey's Country Christmas. But their most unique addition was tacked on in 2011—their annual Garlic and Rockabilly Festival. Along with a line-up of great musical talent, there are cooking demonstrations and a chance for visitors to taste some of the 12 varieties of garlic, "from mild to OMG!" grown on the farm.

If you ask me, Fantasy Farms earns the award for value-added ingenuity.

Popcorn! Candy Apples!

Apples are not native to the prairies. So it seems weird to me that the reason behind the inception of Morden's Corn and

Apple Festival was because the area was designated as Manitoba's "corn and apple belt" in 1925.

As a former Manitoba resident, born and bred, I get the kudos to corn, but apples? Really?

So I had to check it out with Manitoba's Department of Agriculture, Food and Rural Development and sure enough, apples are grown in my home province. That said, the varieties are all hardy cultivars developed at the Morden Arboretum Research Station to withstand adverse weather conditions like early frosts and a short growing season. But I digress…

To formally tip their collective hats to the crops that have helped develop and sustain their economy, the folks down in Morden hosted the first Corn and Apple Festival in 1967. It was initially put on to celebrate the country's centennial, but it was so well received that it continues to grow and draw visitors from around the province. And if you're lucky enough to make your way down there one day, don't forget to buy a jug of the locally brewed apple cider. According to the festival's website, the cider makes the perfect gift, is "wonderful to have around the house for a nice breakfast drink," and can even help "cure…cold bones when warmed." Don't forget the cinnamon stick garnish.

WE CANADIANS KNOW HOW TO PARTY!

A Dickens of a Christmas

The town of Carlyle is located in the southeastern corner of Saskatchewan. Home to almost 1500 people, Carlyle is a typical prairie community dishing up heaping portions of small town hospitality in a flavour of its own making. Take its annual winter festival as an example. Celebrating winter in the typical way just wouldn't do for the residents of Carlyle. Instead, this festival embraces the season with Dickensian inspiration. There are English markets, a Tiny Tim's Taste Tour, High Tea, Carriage Rides and street urchins. But the crowning touch to Canada's only Dickens Village Festival is its annual production of *A Christmas Carol*. Every year the local theatre troupe presents a version of the Victorian classic. And once the curtain falls, patrons can wander on down to Fezziwig's Family Pub and Warming Place for a hot toddy and some free entertainment.

DID YOU  KNOW?

The German tire company Fulda hosts an annual event in Whitehorse, Yukon, that is aptly named The Fulda Challenge. Every year athletes and celebs from Europe participate in unique events like the airplane pulling contest, ice chopping and dog mushing. And while they're at it, the company gets a chance to test how the tires they've created hold up in extreme winter conditions. Seriously. This entire event is all about raising the company's profile. Now I admit I'm not big on tire shopping, but I think the company might need to invest even more money in the public relations department because I've never heard of Fulda tires.

HAUNTED HABITATS

GHOSTLY ENCOUNTERS

It may well be that one day we will be able to prove that the conscious self continues after physical death. If this is truly the case, then there is nothing supernatural or paranormal about it. It will be proven as totally natural and completely normal. It is merely waiting to be discovered.

—Greg Pocha, Director of Paranormal Studies,
Eidolon Project Canada

Although it's hard to put a number on it, the paranormal industry is alive and growing in North America. One study from 2011 suggests that 71 percent of Americans say they've had some kind of paranormal encounter, whether in the form of seeing a ghost, communicating with a deceased loved one or making use of any of the countless other mediums available for such a purpose. In this country, a national survey suggests almost half of all Canadians believe in spirits or ghosts, and 2.5 million Canadians think their home is haunted or "hosts a supernatural presence."

I would like to say I think believing in ghosts is weird, but I've had a few unexplained experiences in my own life that give me pause to think….

What do you think?

Crime of the Century

A visit to London Ontario's Grand Theatre offers patrons a rich array of entertainment options. And if you're lucky, you might catch a sideshow for free! The building's resident spirit, whom many believe is the ghost of the theatre's founder, Ambrose Small, is said to have taken up permanent residence there.

Small was an entrepreneur who purchased a string of small theatres shortly after he got married. The couple were a strange pair. Ambrose was a bit of a player while his wife, Theresa, was a devout Catholic who focused her efforts on good works. Somehow the two managed to make their marriage work for 17 years, but on December 2, 1919, all that changed. Small made a deal to sell his theatres but disappeared shortly after depositing a $1 million cheque into the couple's account at the Dominion Bank. He simply vanished.

The prevailing theory of the day was that Ambrose had been murdered. A number of theories surfaced, ranging from Theresa herself arranging his death after years of frustration at his side to a wronged participant of an earlier business dealing taking his revenge.

But there were other theories about his disappearance, too. In particular, many believed that Ambrose wasn't dead at all, but living well and happily in some exotic location. However and wherever the man met his end, if stories about a ghostly presence wandering the stage of the Grand Theatre prior to a performance or visiting the back stage dressing rooms are any indication, Ambrose Small returned to the theatre he loved. It seems to be where he plans to stay. As for what actually happened to the man the night he disappeared into a wintry Toronto night, not a single solid clue has ever surfaced.

Light and Shadow
Captains and crewmen manoeuvring the Great Lakes in 1808 were undoubtedly overjoyed when the Gibraltar Point Lighthouse became operational. It's been more than

200 years since the lighthouse first cast its beam over the waters of Lake Ontario, safely guiding mariners into Toronto's harbour. A "wooden cage with a fixed whale-oil lantern" originally crowned the hexagon-shaped, a 15.8-metre tall tower constructed of walls that, at the base, measure 1.8 metres thick. The tower was later raised another 9 metres, and its increased size, coupled with a revolving, electronic light, extended the distance its light could travel over the often murky and mysterious waters.

Not long after it began its operations, the lighthouse found itself in the middle of a mystery. John Paul Radelmüller served as its first keeper, taking charge of the task in 1809. But on January 2, 1815, Radelmüller disappeared. Initial attempts to locate him were unsuccessful, and a newspaper story from *The York Gazette*, dated January 14, 1815, stated that Radelmüller was murdered the same night he disappeared. One story suggested that drunken soldiers from Fort York attacked and killed the lighthouse keeper after he refused to sell them beer—it's been suggested Radelmüller supplemented his income by selling bootlegged ale. There is no record of soldiers being tried and found guilty of Radelmüller murder. Unfortunately, it doesn't seem that there were a lot of other leads to pursue.

Legend goes on to suggest that the unfortunate lighthouse keeper's body, or parts of it, were discovered in 1893 when George Durnan, the fourth and arguably longest-standing lighthouse keeper, having served from 1853–1908, claimed he discovered a coffin and a man's jawbone buried in about one metre of sand near his home on the property.

The discovery raised more questions than it answered. If the remains belonged to Radelmüller, why would a murderer take the time to bury them near his home and in a coffin? And what happened to the rest of Radelmüller's body?

Ten keepers manned the lighthouse between 1809 and 1958, when it was decommissioned. But the building is still a beacon for visitors to the Toronto area. The lighthouse is considered the oldest original lighthouse in the country, and one of only three built with its signature hexagonal tower. What some have called Toronto's first unsolved murder adds another layer of interest to the site, as do the stories of Radelmüller's ghost, who has been seen wandering the lighthouse and its grounds.

In 1999, Manuel Cappel took on the task of voluntarily manning the lighthouse. He told writer Dennis Smith it was a labour of love, but one that came with a few unsettling moments. "She's aesthetically and architecturally beautiful. During the day she's serene and welcoming. But at night, she can be downright creepy."

DID YOU KNOW?

Many Canadian cities host ghost tours for the public, and they appear to be growing in popularity. In 2014, more than 155 buildings participated in the annual Doors Open Toronto festival, a citywide celebration of the city's "architecturally, historically, culturally and socially significant buildings." That year's theme—"Secrets and Spirits…Exploring the Mysteries Behind the Door." Ghosts are said to inhabit about 20 of the buildings on the tour, including the Gibraltar Point Lighthouse.

Welcome Youth?

Not only does the Carelton Country Gaol, constructed in 1862, have a history of housing some of this country's most dangerous criminals, it also has the reputation of being haunted. This could be because the jail, located in Ottawa, has been the site of several executions, the last being the hanging of convicted cop killer Eugene Larment in 1946.

By all accounts it was an uncomfortably overcrowded jail, with way too many men, women and, at times, children stuffed into 1 x 3 metre or 2 x 3 metre cells. Even amongst prisons, landing here was scraping the bottom of the barrel! Strange, then, that since it closed in 1972, the jail has been transformed into a…wait for it…youth hostel! Between welcoming young travellers with comfortable beds and free breakfast, the hostel offers free tours of the former jail. The guided walks include ghost tours that pass by the gallows and numerous sites where some of the executed prisoners have allegedly roamed at one time or another over the years.

And the Prize Goes to…

Haunted houses move aside. The folks down in St. John's, Newfoundland, offer those of you who seek out the paranormal something more promising than a single haunted house. They have a haunted street! According to folklore, ghosts have been reported for more than a century in several homes along Victoria Street, one of the oldest streets in St. John's. The LSPU Hall Theatre (named for its previous tenants, the Longshoremen's Protective Union), boasts its own phantom who, some eyewitnesses have suggested, even likes to take in a show every now and again!

A Whopper of a Story

Once can never be too careful, even when it comes to starting a new job. According to a New Brunswick legend, not long after settling in with his new job at a logging camp, situated along the Dungarvon River, a young Irish cook named Ryan met his tragic fate. The young lad, whose appearance has been described as tall, dark and handsome with a strong physique and curly hair, could certainly hold his own in the kitchen. He was a character too—he liked to wake the boys up with a loud whoop and holler.

He also made no secret about the fact that he had money—and it was safely wrapped around his waist in his money belt.

One day there was a new camp boss on site, and he elected to stay back while his men went off logging. This was strange but not unheard of. What the men discovered on their return was completely unexpected, however. Ryan was dead! One version of the story suggests they discovered his lifeless body on the floor, minus his money belt. Of course none of this surprised the boss, who simply said Ryan had fallen ill and died.

Perhaps the men were too afraid to ask what happened to Ryan's money belt. When the boss told the men to bury the young man in the neighbouring woods, no one questioned him; they just followed orders.

That night Mother Nature had no problem letting her thoughts on the matter be known. The winds howled, drilling torrential rains on the camp and its occupants. And over the sounds of the storm could be heard mournful cries and whooping sounds that many attributed to the distressed spirit of the murdered man.

Frightened, the woodsmen at the camp pulled up stakes and left. However, that didn't put an end to wild sounds heard in the area. The sounds were so distressing that it's been said a Roman Catholic priest from a nearby community was called in to try and calm the spirit with words from the Bible and a blessing. There are differing views on whether or not this worked.

The story of the Dungarvon Whopper continues to intrigue New Brunswickers and visitors to the Atlantic province. Songs and plays have been written about the legendary spirit, and a passenger train that runs between Newcastle and Fredericton has been nicknamed in its honour.

Bell Island Anomalies

At an area of roughly 34 square kilometres, Bell Island is a tidy parcel of chiselled shoreline located in Conception Bay, Newfoundland and Labrador. The first European settlers were fishermen and farmers, arriving in the 18th century, but during its heyday, Bell Island was best known as a mining capital of the coast. No one really knows how much iron ore could be pulled up from the site, but for seven decades, until the mines closed in 1966, underground operations covered more than

180 square kilometres. However, it's the ethereal qualities of this island haven that have kept Bell Island in the public eye throughout the generations.

Tragic death resulting in lost love is at the core of one prevailing ghost story. The tale tells of a horrible mining accident in 1933 that resulted in the death of a young man, and how after his death, his widow walked every day to the tunnel entrance at his regular quitting time, praying she'd wake up from the nightmare that changed her life forever. Then suddenly, one day, he seemed to emerge from the tunnel. Maybe it was a dream. Or maybe the man's spirit was so troubled by his widow's grief that he reached out from the beyond to try and comfort her.

Other deaths have occurred at Mine #2 as well, and other ghostly apparitions of the deceased have been reported. Another Bell Island legend has its basis in the banshee of Irish folklore. The setting: Dobbin's Gardens and its surrounding marshes. The problem: a spirit that appears most often as a bent, crippled old hag. Her appearance is supposed to be an omen of an impending death, but she's also known to stalk any man walking through the marsh.

Lift Your Spirits?
The Newman Wine Vaults in St. John's houses an assortment of bubbly, along with a few spirits of another flavour—the otherworldly kind. According to some sources, everything from the ghost of a baby to that of a slave have been seen at different times on the premises.

Pace, Turn, Fire

Duelling as a way to settle conflicts was at one time commonplace. Typically, a duel resulted in the death of one of the two participants, but in some cases unforeseen repercussions kept the conflict alive in perpetuity.

Such was the case with the last conflict decided by a legal duel in what is now Canada. The duel occurred near St. John's, Newfoundland.

The two men involved are only remembered as one Mr. Dooley and one Mr. Healey. They had been fast friends their entire lives, until they had the unfortunate luck to fall in love with the same woman, whose name appears to be lost to history. One variation of the story suggests the two men got cold feet. They initially went ahead with their plan and began pacing away from each other, and at the appropriate point they stopped, turned and fired, but Dooley fainted from fear and Healey was horrified at the thought that he killed his good friend over a girl. As it turned out, the men's seconds—the friends each man had chosen to attempt to mediate their dispute and ensure a duel, should it indeed take place, was conducted fairly—had conspired against Dooley and Healey and replaced their bullets with blanks. In this version of the story, everyone was admittedly relieved with the outcome. No mention was made of any decision regarding the young lady in question.

A second story named as the last legal duel in Newfoundland doesn't go into the same details as the account above. Details are sketchy at best. But what has made its way into ghostly folklore is that a duel occurred near St. John's and, in this version, someone died. It appears the loser of this conflict was not a gracious loser. For the better part of two centuries residents have reported seeing a man holding a gun and sporting a bullet hole in his head. And almost as soon as he's seen, the apparition vanishes into thin air.

Are these two stories different versions of the same tale? Has time and our human tendency to adapt stories to our liking created the happy, or the tragic, ending? Regardless of your take on the story, the apparition of a mortally wounded man continues haunting that corner of the country.

New Digs?
Talk about repurposing old items. A bizarre story from Atlantic Canada comes to us via the Canadian television series *Creepy Canada*. In its second season, reporters from the show shared the tale of a St. John's bistro called Chez Brian. Apparently this dining establishment had been known to serve up more than an abundance of tasty treats for the palate. If you're lucky—or not, depending on your point of view—dinner there might afford you a peak at one of several ghosts said to inhabit the building.

Now you might think the ghosts wandered in from a neighbouring haunt, but that doesn't seem to be the case. They are thought to be former inhabitants of the building, which was once—wait for it—a mortuary! Among the spirits said to wander this restaurant are a strange man placing coins on the eyes of what appears to be a paralyzed woman and another lady sporting a jagged scar down her torso. Now isn't that appetizing?

As an aside, you might find it interesting to hear that try as I might, I cannot locate a Chez Brian in St. John's, Newfoundland, online. It appears these apparitions put a sour taste in the mouths of potential diners.

A Ghost of Higher Learning
If you are beginning to suspect Atlantic Canada has the corner on this country's ghosts, think again. The University of

Toronto boasts a wide assortment of ghosts. In fact, the campus is so haunted that Richard Fiennes-Clinton, founder of Muddy York Walking Tours, designed a ghost tour specifically for the U of T. In an article that appeared in the student newspaper *The Varsity*, in September 2012, Fiennes-Clinton explained that some of the ghosts inhabiting the campus once lived in the area, which used to be a residential neighbourhood, while others were connected with the university itself.

Eerie little girls in pretty white dresses and the occasional psychopath aside, what many consider the most persistent ghost of the bunch resides at Trinity College, and was once an Anglican bishop as well as the man who founded the university. What many believe to be the ghost of John Strachan has been seen strolling the hallways decked out in his bishop robes. His appearance most often coincides with the anniversary of his death, and those who are familiar with his overbearing nature have suggested the man known for his somewhat imperious rule can't rest in peace without checking in to ensure everything is still in good working order.

Betrayed Love

This tragedy began, like many others, as a love story. And as with most other good legends, there are several variations.

Let's begin with the characters as we know them. The conflict took place between two stonemasons: Ivan Reznikoff, a large Slavic man of rough features, and a Greek man named Paul Diabolos. Both men were working on the construction of the University of Toronto's University College building, which was under construction from 1856 to 1859. The object of their conflict—one lovely lady known in some retellings of this story as Susie, the daughter of a local publican.

Susie and Reznikoff were engaged, and Reznikoff was earnestly saving for their impending marriage when he discovered the love of his life had also been stepping out with Diabolos. In some versions of the story, a cocky Diabolos boasted about the girl's disloyalty to Reznikoff, while in other renditions Reznikoff catches the two in a lovers' embrace, plotting to run off together (with the money Reznikoff had been saving).

However it began, the two men ended up in a bitter fight to the death, with a much larger, stronger Reznikoff wielding a two-headed axe while Diabolos attempted to defend himself with his dagger. In one version of the tale it's Reznikoff—the wronged man—who is murdered at the hand of his rival, his body unceremoniously tossed down an unfinished staircase and later entombed in the unfinished building. Other versions of the tale speak of Reznikoff as a drunken brute that would have no doubt mistreated young Susie, had the two actually married. And in some scenarios a frightened Diabolos tried to hide from Reznikoff. In the middle of their struggle Diabolos ducked, trying to avoid Reznikoff's swinging axe. Losing his balance, Reznikoff plunged to his death, making it neither murder nor self-defence, but an accident.

No one knew for sure what became of the burly Russian. But within a decade or so of his disappearance, rumours began to circulate that Reznikoff's ghost had been seen wandering the campus, telling anyone who would listen about his earthly plight. Then on February 14, 1890, a fire erupted on the east stairway where Reznikoff was said to have died, and human remains were discovered. Although the remains were never positively identified as Reznikoff, even diehard skeptics began to believe the tale.

Visions in White

The beautiful Banff Springs Hotel has everything you'd ever want in a vacation getaway. It even has a few resident ghosts, including a ghost bride, to keep you on your toes. And it's not the only hotel with such a claim. Winnipeg's stately Fort Garry Hotel has a few ethereal residents of its own, including a ghost bride. Based on MacDonald's tale, it appears no clear-cut answers about Cawdor's death were discovered.

The story about each of these brides is quite different, but equally tragic. The ghost bride of Banff Springs died when her gown caught fire on the candles lighting the spiral staircase, or as the result of a fall, depending on which version of the story you read. In the Winnipeg tragedy, an inconsolable bride commits suicide after learning her new husband was killed in a car accident.

DID YOU  KNOW?

Reports of otherworldly activities are so prevalent in British Columbia that those interested in the paranormal have developed a well-established group known as the British Columbia Ghosts and Hauntings Research Society. This non-profit, volunteer-run society collects, records and researches stories of strange happenings throughout the province. And if they need help from other, more experienced paranormal researchers, they can turn to the Canadian pros in the field from PSICAN (Paranormal Studies and Investigations Canada), which has been around since March 2005.

Calling all Spirits

At least one ghost wanders the ruins of Silver Islet. A reclusive miner named James Cawdor admitted to hearing the voice of a dead miner informing him of the location of a cache of silver nuggets and the best way to retrieve them. The next day Cawdor didn't come home. The following week, his body was discovered floating in a water-filled shaft. Because there was no indication that he purposefully made his way to the shaft, there were whispers that Cawdor may have been pushed, or simply fallen, to his death. His home was boarded up. For several of his family members, the story didn't end with his death. They wanted one last chance to speak with their loved one and hopefully get some answers about how he might have died.

Enter the renowned Sir Arthur Conan Doyle. Along with being the creator of Sherlock Holms, Doyle was also something of a spiritualist. He travelled Canada widely and frequently. It was in 1914, after Doyle gave a talk at the Colonial Theatre in neighbouring Port Arthur, that he was approached by Cawdor's stepdaughter, who wanted to tempt the writer into hosting a séance so she could speak with her deceased father. Intrigued, as any good mystery writer would be, Doyle jumped at the chance.

Initially the pair met at Cawdor's gravesite, but when nothing transpired, Doyle suggested they hold a séance at night at Cawdor's home. The problem was that Doyle was about to leave Silver Islet, so the séance would have to take place at another time.

The war postponed what was going to be a much earlier visit, and it wasn't until nine years later in 1923 that Doyle returned to the area. This time they met at night at Cawdor's abandoned home, as they had discussed, and the results were far more productive. The sounds of rattling hinges, jingled chains and other appropriately frightening noises filled the room before Doyle called to Cawdor and told him of his daughter's need to speak with him. A dialogue ensued between father and daughter—a dialogue that Doyle witnessed but the daughter did not remember after the séance.

Doyle's visit to Silver Islet was big news. Being a fan of the Shelock Holmes mysteries, I was thrilled to learn of it during my visit there in the 1990s. More recently, Bill MacDonald chronicled the story in the magazine *Geist*; Cawdor's daughter was his aunt. Based on MacDonald's tale, it seems no answers about Cawdor's death were discovered.

A Mind of Her Own

The James Bay Inn, located in historic Victoria, BC, is a stately establishment with a colourful history. Although it was built as a hotel, it operated as St. Mary's Priory from 1942 to 1945. During that time, Canadian artist Emily Carr fell ill and spent her last days there. According to one legend, once the building was used again as a hotel, the ghost of Emily Carr would appear in a particular men's washroom. In fact, she frequented that bathroom so often that the sightings made the local newspaper. It's been said that a clipping of the news story, along with Carr's photograph, at one time hung on the men's washroom door.

Did You Say Something?

A small, limestone tunnel originally built in the early 1900s as drainage for farmlands in the Niagara Falls area runs beneath what was once the Grand Trunk Railway. Farmers also used the tunnel to transport goods or animals. And if asked, just about everyone who knows of the tunnel would agree the 38-metre long passageway is spooky. Some have even claimed they've heard a woman's screams echo through the tunnel from time to time.

As luck would have it, an equally spooky story or two accompanies every unexplained scream. At least three local legends could have fuelled people's imaginations in that regard. One story tells of a young girl who died in the tunnels after trying to escape a fire; her tortured spirit continues to try and find its way to the light. Another version of the story, a particularly distasteful version as weird stories go, suggests an estranged father purposely set the girl on fire, reacting to a custody battle and divorce proceedings. A third theory is equally abhorrent. It tells of how a young girl had been raped in the tunnel and then set on fire. If you are the sort of person who believes in ghosts, you'd likely agree that any of these stories is motivation for a ghostly presence there.

Land of the Midnight Sun

Gold Rush fever lured men by the thousands to the land of the midnight sun. Even cold temperatures and treacherous geography couldn't dissuade them from scouring the landscape for the mother lode. But these adventurous souls were often woefully unprepared for the brutal conditions.

That's what, legend suggests, happened to one prospector who found himself and his pack of dogs lost, cold and unsure of which direction to take. The prospector gave in for the night and fell into a deep, uneasy sleep that culminated in a dream of a warrior threatening him with death unless he left. The prospector said he'd be glad to leave if only he knew the way out of the muskeg where he'd found himself.

The prospector's reply seemed reasonable to the warrior, who was now faced with a dilemma. He couldn't very well leave his post as protector of the land to escort the lost miner to safety. Instead, he delegated the task, and the prospector woke to find the ghostly image of a Native woman beckoning to him. Even the dogs must have recognized the ghost's good intentions for, according to the story, they stopped growling at the apparition and hastened to follow. Not one to argue, the prospector followed suit.

At one point, the "woman" transformed into a snow-white hare, leaping effortlessly as it led the way. Before too long the man and his dogs found themselves on familiar ground, and they parted company with the spirit, which by now had returned to its previous state as a beautiful Native woman.

Disaster in Paradise

Charlie Dupres was a fun-loving fellow who enjoyed the outdoors and loved to ski. So when a road was built linking what's now the Icefields Parkway to Marmot Basin, Charlie was one of the first skiers in what is now Jasper National Park to take advantage of the new road to hit the slopes. Sadly, he's remembered for a darker contribution to Alberta's history; on March 11, 1955, Dupres was the first skier to be killed by an avalanche in the area. To honour his memory, two runs at Marmot Basin were named after him: Dupres Bowl and Charlie's Bowl.

But Charlie wasn't content with being remembered only by his namesakes. Although his body was deceased, his spirit remained very much alive. And it's believed the man, known for being a jokester in life, continues to trick visitors and staff at the Eagle Chalet where his equipment remains on display in Charlie's Lounge.

Weyburn Mental Hospital

At the height of its operations, the Weyburn Mental Hospital, located in Weyburn, Saskatchewan, housed as many as 2500 patients. Established in 1921, there's no doubt the facility, which was a huge building considered to be one of the largest in the British Empire, offered support for many clients and an increased understanding of mental health issues at that time in Canadian history. Early methods of therapy at the Weyburn Hospital included recreational opportunities like dancing and music. But that wasn't all the hospital offered. Other techniques, such as electroshock therapy, lobotomies and even LSD experiments, were consider by many as questionable practices that had frightening results.

The problem wasn't just about the techniques being used, which many sources claim were done with the best of intentions despite the fact that many negative ramifications resulted from these practices. Another problem with the hospital was that it became a drop-off spot for families with members who had other health-related problems, such as a stroke, for example. That kind of situation led to overcrowding and made things increasingly difficult for staff to deal with patients. And some researchers have suggested these factors resulted in the halls of Weyburn Hospital being haunted by apparitions, sounds and poltergeist-like happenings. In particular, a ghostly woman was seen wandering the fourth floor of the hospital.

The original hospital was demolished by 2009, but not before several attempts were made to sell it to clients interested in renovating and repurposing it. It's unclear if the ghosts said to inhabit the hospital caused these potential sales to fall through. But what is certain is the resident ghosts have been forced to move on to other quarters, or were perhaps released to a more peaceful existence.

HAUNTED HABITATS

ANIMATING THE INANIMATE

Viking Ghost Ship
John Cabot may have been the first explorer commissioned by England to land on the rocky shores of Newfoundland and begin charting the territory during his expedition of 1497, but others had visited The Rock long before. Norse navigators first found their way to what would become Newfoundland and Labrador around 1006, almost 500 years before Cabot. The Vikings established a small village, now called L'Anse aux Meadows, at the northernmost tip of the island. L'Anse aux Meadows wasn't actually discovered until 1960, and then quite by accident. It is now UNESCO World Heritage site.

Some say the Vikings have never truly left the area. Residents along that part of the coast have reported seeing a ship that looks like a Viking ship, with its characteristic large central sail and dragon's head pointing the way at the bow. Without exception, the sightings are always in June, and as if to ensure no one misses its appearance, the ship has been known to blow its horn late at night. What's even more eerie is that when the Viking boat makes its ghostly appearance in Newfoundland, Icelandic residents living on the southwest corner of their country have reported seeing a strange ship leaving their coastline at the same time.

Eyewitness Error

The first reference to the famous Canadian maritime oddity known as the "Phantom Ship" dates back to 1786 after several eyewitnesses reported seeing a burning ship floating across the Northumberland Strait, which separates PEI from New Brunswick and Nova Scotia. This body of water is about 210 kilometres long, but depending on where you're situated along that expanse, its width can vary between 12 and 48 kilometres, meaning that witnesses can easily watch any ships passing by.

The vantage point of a lighthouse makes it even easier to see what's going on at sea, and it was a keeper at Sea Cow Head who first recorded seeing the three-masted schooner sailing aimlessly toward the rocky shore before disappearing. Other sightings describe the ship in flames, and some report crew-members or passengers attempting to escape the conflagration by leaping into the ocean. One account of such a sighting comes from the Charlottetown Harbour in the early 1900s. That sighting was allegedly so convincing that a rescue attempt was made, but the ship disappeared from view before its would-be rescue party ever reached it. Although there are variations to the stories that have circulated about the Phantom Ship through the centuries, the shocking similarities among them are far greater than the points where they diverge.

People still report seeing the ghostly vessel from time to time. One of the more recent witness reports was chronicled in the *Truro Daily News* on February 23, 2008. According to the article penned by Sherry Martell, 17-year-old Mathieu Giguere noticed a "brightly lit ship" in Tatamagouch Bay. At first he didn't think much of what he saw since it wasn't unusual for cruise ships to pass by at night. But then he realized it was February; the bay was full of ice, making any kind of boat traffic unlikely. He also remembered the ship didn't look anything like a cruise ship, but rather like the *Bluenose*. Because the young man wasn't from the area, he wasn't familiar with the legend of the Phantom Ship. It was a local resident who regaled Giguere with the story after hearing what the young man had seen.

Ghostly Locomotive

The stretch of railway track running north and south of St. Louis, Saskatchewan, was torn up decades ago, but that doesn't stop a train from ploughing through the prairie every so often. Countless witnesses claim to have seen the light of a train travelling north into town.

There are at least two stories explaining the existence of this ghostly presence. The first, and perhaps most prevalent, is that a conductor was once beheaded on the line during the performance of a routine check, and his restless ghost still rides the rails.

The second version of the story seems more plausible in that it involves an engineer, and it would follow that a ghostly engineer would more likely drive a train than a conductor. In any case, in this version the engineer in question was at the helm when the train he was driving wiped out an entire family. He was so distraught as a result of the accident that he committed suicide. Unfortunately, his death didn't assuage his grief, and as the story goes, he continues to ride the rails to this day.

It has been suggested distant car headlights are responsible for the ghost train phenomenon. The theory was tested throughout the years and refuted, but in 2009, two grade 12 students from La Ronge decided to test the hypothesis for a school science fair project. They theorized that cars travelling with their headlights on along roadways that lined up with the now defunct railway line could be responsible for the sightings. The father of one of the girls helped them test the theory by flashing his headlights at various locations they'd plotted on a map. Unfortunately the girls, stationed at the location where most of the sightings took place and monitoring communication with their helper via cell phone, couldn't see the lights.

Undeterred, the girls decided to test roads at a higher elevation. After trying several locations, they hit pay dirt when one small stretch of highway produced the results they were looking for—they saw the car lights flashing. As far as the girls were concerned, people seeing car lights from that location could have mistaken them for the headlights of a train. They further discovered that although the car's headlights would have been too small to see at such a distance, their light could have been diffracted or their beam expanded when emitted through a small opening, such as a ridge or groove in the landscape or a space in a clump of trees.

Although the girls aced their science experiment and were satisfied with their results, diehard believers don't accept that the findings explain every sighting. Certainly, some sightings could have resulted from an optical illusion, but it didn't seem reasonable to suggest that small portion of roadway could have the kind of traffic volume necessary to produce the number of sightings reported. The girls' findings also didn't explain the fact that the kinds of lights viewed in various accounts differed, and that some of these sightings occurred long before motorized vehicles with headlights, or the roads for them to travel on, existed.

And so it goes that the legend of the St. Louis ghost train lives on in local folklore, and in the minds of residents and visitors alike, minus two new graduates with a newsworthy science fair project.

Living Doll?

Did you know that Canada has its own version of Chucky, the star of the slasher horror movie *Child's Play?* Mandy the Haunted Doll made its appearance at the Quesnel Museum in 1991 after its previous owner donated it. That owner, a woman known only as Mereanda, was repeatedly awakened in the middle of the night by the sound of a baby crying. When she searched for the origin of the sounds, she'd discover an open window near the doll. Eventually she decided the doll was the cause of her problems, and because it was an antique, she thought it best to donate it to the BC museum rather than discard it or drop it off at a second-hand store. As expected, once she rid herself of the doll, she was also spared the nightly terror of babies crying beside mysteriously opened windows.

Although the donor's problem appeared to be solved, museum staff now had a new donation with a questionable history. Mandy's origins were anything but clear, but historians agreed she was likely created in Germany, sometime between 1910 and 1920. The doll's travels from the time she was created until she landed in Mereanda's hands were unknown, but her presence clearly stressed Mereanda and, as chance would have it, the doll would prove challenging for museum staff as well. Aside from the gashes or cracks on her face, Mandy looks charming, but those who have seen her in person, or experienced some of the strange "powers" she's credited with, might describe her as anything but.

Of course Quesnel Museum staff didn't expect any trouble when they accepted the doll as a donation. Any silly notions of a potential possession were just that, silly. It was easy to dismiss the claims, but when lunches started disappearing from the refrigerator only to be discovered elsewhere, and other strange things began happening, thoughts about the doll changed. Eventually, museum staff moved Mandy from her position at the museum's entryway, where she sometimes spooked patrons, to her own display case in the hope that she wouldn't cause as much of a disruption. But Mandy continues to bewilder staff and visitors alike with quirky little surprises. Some visitors have reported that the doll makes them feel sad, while others say their electronics have fizzled out when they were around her.

News of Mandy has flooded media outlets throughout BC and spread across Canada. You never know what you'll find when you visit the strange doll at the Quesnel Museum, but for a lot of folks that's the draw. Maybe it's even enough for you to take a trip down the Old Cariboo Gold Rush Trail to check it out for yourself.

A WALK ON THE WILD SIDE

SEEING IS BELIEVING?

One thing to remember is to talk to the animals. If you do, they will talk back to you. But if you don't talk to the animals, they won't talk back to you, then you won't understand, and when you don't understand, you will fear and when you fear you will destroy the animals, and if you destroy the animals, you will destroy yourself.

–Chief Dan George, Chief of the Tsleil-Waututh Nation, British Columbia

In a country where wide-open spaces and wilderness reign, rare is the Canadian who hasn't had at least one encounter with a wild animal during his or her lifetime. My first close encounter happened at the ripe old age of four. My much older sister Heather and I were sitting on a log in front of our family's trailer at White Lake, Manitoba, chatting it up with her boyfriend when he suddenly stopped talking and warned us that there was a bear walking toward us. Used to his kibitzing, Heather laughed him off. But he insisted. So I decided to check it out. When I stood up, I saw a large black bear approaching us. When I informed my sister that her boyfriend was quite accurate in his warning, she didn't stick around to get acquainted with the furry creature.

Black bears are among the more common creatures roaming this vast country. But there are other less common critters creeping about—critters that, should they be spotted in your neck of the woods, might keep you sleeping with one eye open.

Making a Big Impression

I remember the first time I wandered into Banff's Natural History Museum and stood nose to navel with the statue of a sasquatch replica. Because I was a '60s child and a woodland wanderer in my own right, the legend of a hairy creature roaming the wilds of North America captured my attention. I was equally awed and frightened. What if it was real, and I happened upon one of these sleeping giants during one of my wilderness excursions?

Stories of a bipedal, humanoid creature who looks like a giant, hairy man or the Chewbacca of *Star Wars* and wanders the forests of this continent have been circulating for centuries. And although the description of such a creature is typically uniform, it has gone by various names. For example, the Native Coast Salish of BC called the creature a *sokqueatle* or *sos-a'tal*. It was a Canadian schoolteacher named J.W. Burns who is credited with coming up with the name "sasquatch" to serve as a kind of generic term for all the "wild man" sightings in North America.

Sources generally agree that although First Nations peoples have legends of the sasquatch that date back before European settlement in Canada, the first recorded European sighting in this country took place in what is now Jasper National Park. In 1811, during his quest to find the mouth of the Columbia River, David Thompson discovered what appeared to be a strange large footprint in the snow near what is now the town of Jasper. The print was 35 centimetres long, 20 centimetres wide, sported four toes with short claws and left a deep impression by the ball and heel. It was because of the large imprints reported in several accounts that the creature was given its nickname, Big Foot. In his journals, Thompson suggested the imprint could have been "the track of a large old grizzled bear," but then adds his doubts on that conclusion.

It took prospector Albert Ostman 33 years to report what he saw in 1924. Ostman said he'd been working near Toba Inlet, BC, when he was abducted, sleeping bag and all, by a large male sasquatch and held captive by what appeared to be a family of the creatures for several days before he escaped. While stories of sasquatch sightings weren't uncommon, they were usually dismissed as cases of mistaken identity, hoaxes or figments of overactive imaginations. Perhaps that's why Ostman seemed reluctant to report his experience, which, by the way, was eventually considered to be "more likely the result of imagination than of recollection."

Sasquatch sightings have been reported in every part of Canada, but the vast majority come from British

Columbia—apparently our Big Foot loves the mountains and the vast expanse of undeveloped land they offer. Yet critics are quick to point out that stories of the creature are all we have to go on—there isn't one shred of evidence, not one unidentifiable hair, no bones, no corpse, nothing concrete to support the claim that such a creature exists outside the imagination of the few who claim to have seen it. For those people, and for others who care to believe, the mystery will live on until the day that evidence is unearthed.

And they have no doubt that day will come.

Prehistoric Predator

For some, water monsters captivate the imagination and instill fear like no other. Based on legends of sea creatures from around the world, they are among the most elusive beasts, and that unpredictability breeds added layers of apprehension. Canada has its fair share of water monsters, and British Columbia is home to one such creature, which some theorize has survived from prehistoric times. And while many may argue there's no physical evidence to support the existence of Big Foot, the same can't be said for Prince Rupert's sea serpent.

More than 300 sightings of a giant, serpent-like creature with many humps, similar to Scotland's famous Loch Ness Monster, Nessie, have been reported along BC's Pacific coast and as far south as the northern tip of California. Some scientists through the years have suggested that Prince Rupert's sea serpent was a cadborosaurus, or "Caddy" as it has affectionately become known. The main difference between Caddy and others of a similar description is that Caddy is believed to have long, webbed hind flippers forming a fan-like tail that propels the creature through the waters at breakneck speed.

The scientific community of the day was certainly skeptical of multiple sightings of a sea creature in the early 1930s. However, the residents of Prince Rupert, BC, had their doubts washed away in the fall of 1934 after a partially decomposed carcass was discovered on the sandy beaches of Henry Island, just south of the port city.

The find sparked interest across the continent. According to an article that appeared in the *Galveston Daily News*, the creature, who was thought to have been dead for about two months at the time of its discovery, measured 9 metres in length. It was described as having "skin like sandpaper, a head resembling that of a horse and a hide partly covered by hair and partly by spines or quills." Although only two fins remained on the carcass, it was determined that when the creature was alive, it would have had four.

Earlier sightings of similar sea serpents farther south, near Vancouver Island, were reported in the *Victoria Times* and the *Victoria Daily Colonist,* and it was speculated that the creature was a cadborosaurus. But scientists weighing in on the subject were inconclusive, suggesting the sightings may have been everything from a prehistoric creature that survived from the Mesozoic age to a basking shark, the second largest fish on record, which often reaches lengths of 10 metres. A photograph is on file at the Prince Rupert City and Regional Archives, its caption indicating the likelihood that the carcass was a basking shark. But there are problems with that theory, too. Basking sharks have more than four fins, and seasoned fishermen who claimed to have sighted the creature in the water would have most likely recognized it as a shark.

Freshwater Enigma

Seas and oceans aren't the only bodies of water that are home to sea monsters. A long, serpent-like creature is said to have inhabited Lake Okanagan since the Salish First Nations first camped on its sandy shore. They called the lake monster with the snake-like body, the head of a horse and little or no tail Naitaka (N'ha-a-itk) or Lake Devil. We now call it Ogopogo. Sightings of the elusive Ogopogo, which are inconsistent in their reporting of the creature's length and estimate the size anywhere from 6 to 20 metres long, were reported on land and in the water. Folklore suggests it had a lair in a cave at Squally Point, near Rattlesnake Island, located on the east shore of the lake across from Peachland. According to legend, the creature had such a reputation that the Salish would not canoe near the area without an offering of some kind of small animal for the Lake Devil. If an offering wasn't made, it wasn't uncommon for a storm to suddenly hit and for the choppy waters, perhaps stirred by the angry serpent's tail, to claim another life.

It's widely believed that, in 1872, Mrs. Susan Allison made the first documented sighting by a Caucasian. In 1947, a Mr. Kray was one of several witnesses who saw the monster from a boat. He described Ogopogo as having "a long sinuous body, 30 feet in length, consisting of about five undulations, apparently separated from each other by about a 2-foot space, in which that part of the undulations would have been underwater. There appeared to be a forked tail, of which only one-half came above the water. From time to time the whole thing submerged and came up again."

At one point cryptozoologist Roy T. Mackal theorized Ogopogo might be an "aquatic fish-eating animal," and later decided the creature was likely a descendant of Basilosaurus cetoides, a prehistoric whale. Over the years, expeditions to find and film Ogopogo have been conducted, and their efforts have been filmed for television stations such as the Discovery Channel. Everyone has a theory about the origins of Canada's most famous lake monster. But it appears most agree about one thing—Ogopogo isn't the Lake Devil the Salish feared. Instead, it seems to be a shy, harmless creature that needs protecting. And in 1989, in an effort to protect Ogopogo from any misguided acts of violence, Bruce Strachan, Minister of the Environment, enacted legislation making it illegal to harm, capture or disturb Ogopogo.

A sign at Lake Okanagan erected by the Department of Recreation and Conservation claims that not a year goes by without a resident or tourist spotting Ogopogo. In 2000, in an effort to put Penticton on the map, Chamber of Commerce manager John Singleton initiated a contest challenging anyone to find definitive proof that Ogopogo exists. The prize for that solid evidence—$2,000,000 in cold hard cash. There was no mention if this prize was ever collected.

Internet sites documenting Ogopogo sightings are evidence that the public continues to take an active interest in the lake monster mystery. Of course, others suggest the story is nothing more than an ancient legend propagated by the imaginations and wishful thinking of local residents. Those who've seen Ogopogo with their own eyes would beg to differ.

Champion Cryptid

Canada's Lake Champlain shares its lake monster with our American neighbours in Vermont and New York, and the more than 300 reported sightings of the creature have boosted tourism all around that lake. In 1609, a member of French explorer Samuel de Champlain's expedition recorded one of the first written accounts of a lake creature inhabiting the depths of Lake Champlain. However, legends of Champ originated long before that with the Iroquois and Abenaki First Nations; the Abenaki called the lake monster Tatoskok. It wasn't uncommon for members of these First Nations tribes to offer gifts or sacrifices to the creature, but it doesn't appear these gifts were given to appease an angry monster. In fact, most accounts say that Champ is shy and prefers to avoid contact with the public.

A description from 1819 called Champ an "enormous serpentine monster." Joseph W. Zarzynski, founder of Lake Champlain Phenomena Investigation, suggests that in about one-third of the reports, Champ is described as being dark skinned, between 4 and 7 metres long, with one or more humps. However, some reports suggest the creature could measure anywhere from 3 to 60 metres. Perhaps that means there is more than one Champ living in these waters, adding another layer to the mystery?

Some have suggested that Champ might be a prehistoric creature that survived the ice age; others posit the lake creature might actually be a primitive whale; and still others suggest Champ might be a giant lake sturgeon or unknown species of eel.

As with other water monsters, search teams have descended on the large lake, using everything from echolocation to underwater photography to prove Champ's existence. If Champ is actually located, great care will need to be taken so as not to injure it in any way, as both New York and Vermont have declared the creature a protected species.

New Kid on the Block

In 2009, after decades of reported sightings of a large creature rising to the surface of Cameron Lake, researchers with the BC Scientific Cryptozoology Club set out to tour the inland waters. Using a fish finder they were able to identify several items they estimated were about "30 or 40 pounds in size, or possibly multiple items in excess of that size." Investigators did note the items they recorded could later be identified as sturgeon, eel, or very large trout. To date, the identity of the Cameron Lake monster remains a mystery.

DID YOU KNOW?

Aside from Ogopogo and Champ, Canada boasts several other, lesser-known lake monsters:

- the Thetis Lake monster in Thetis Lake, BC
- Manitoba's Manipogo of Lake Manitoba and Winnipogo of Lake Winnipegosis
- the Lake Utopia Lake Monster in New Brunswick

- Cressie of Crescent Lake, Newfoundland
- Ontario's Igopogo of Lake Simcoe, Mussie of Muskrat Lake, Mishipeshu of Lake Superior and Kingstie of Lake Ontario
- Mugwump of Lake Temiskaming and Memphre of Lake Memphremagog in Québec
- a nameless monster in Reindeer Lake, Saskatchewan, which is said to burst through the ice during the winter to capture any animals passing by
- and a monster in Alberta's Lac Ste Anne that inspired local residents to call the lake Devil's Lake.

Newfie Notable

The kraken is a sea monster of mythic proportions, the mention of which struck fear into the heart of even the most rugged sailor as far back as the late 14th century. The giant creature is named for the Norwegian and Swedish word *krake,* referring to an unhealthy or twisted animal. It certainly wasn't healthy for any ship's crew happening upon such a creature, which purportedly boasted long and powerful tentacles capable of capturing and toppling any ship passing overhead.

While legend suggests this sea monster lives along the waters of Norway and Greenland, several stories of a kraken, or a similar sea creature, being captured by Atlantic fishermen off the coast of Newfoundland have circulated for generations. In March 2010, a story in St. John's newspaper *The Telegram* described an unknown aquatic dweller that became tangled in the nets of some fishermen. Trinity Bay fisherman John Marsh said his son and nephew called him up one day in the summer of 2009 to help cut something out of their net. The men thought they'd caught a whale, but Marsh didn't agree. For one thing the creature's neck was 2.5 to 3 metres long, and it didn't have a blowhole like a whale. Marsh also pointed out the carcass was smooth, devoid of barnacles or scratches, as if it had come from fresh water instead of the ocean. Marsh didn't have a camera with him, and by the time he returned to photograph the carcass, the ocean had reclaimed it.

While his story garnered a lot of interest, without pictures or a sample of the carcass, scientists with the Department of Fisheries and Oceans couldn't begin to make an educated guess on what the creature might have been.

"I would have loved to have seen what it was…I love mysteries," researcher Jack Lawson told *The Telegram*. "If it were a new species it would be really exciting…"

Lawson went on to explain that large whales or sharks can decompose to a point where they aren't easily recognizable, even by trained scientists, and DNA testing is needed to determine for certain the identity of these carcasses. Lawson also suggested the carcass could have been a cadborosaurus of BC fame, but when he was shown a picture of Caddy, Marsh said it didn't look the same as the carcass his son and nephew discovered.

Marsh's account is just one of many stories of strange marine life tangled in nets, swimming at the water's surface or washing up on the shores of the Grand Banks of Newfoundland and Labrador. Some tales are generations old while others, like the accounts of a enigma named Cressie who has appeared in Crescent Lake to a couple of men who mistakenly thought the monster was an upturned boat, are relatively recent. And yet to this day, exactly what these creatures are remains a mystery.

The French Connection

Although this monster has been seen throughout North America, and there are variations to the spelling of its name, the *loup-garou* always has connections to francophone cultures, and our Canadian *loup-garou* is no exception.

Basically, a *loup-garou* is a werewolf—a human, usually a man, who morphs into a wolf. Stories of men changing into wolves date back to ancient Greece, but what makes the *loup-garou* different from the typical werewolf is that it can change from human to werewolf at will, and it retains its human faculties while adopting the heightened senses and strength of a wolf. Its ability to shape shift is also not dictated by the cycles of the moon.

There are differing details in the many versions of the *loup-garou* legend. Some suggest that a person must never speak of an encounter with the man-monster lest they themselves turn into one. Others propose the theory that a victim often knows the *loup-garou* that attacked them—perhaps someone with a grudge, like a jealous lover. Another source suggests that someone who kills a *loup-garou* must himself live as a *loup-garou* for 101 days.

A CBC Radio story suggests that in Canada's early history, the Catholic clergy used the legends of a man-beast to frighten wayward parishioners into making better life choices. Perhaps this is why yet another source states the legend of the *loup-garou* was often used to discipline children—misbehave and the *loup-garou* will find you!

Of course, threats of a mysterious man-wolf wouldn't hold any weight had there not been something to inspire the stories in the first place. The first accounts of a werewolf sighting anywhere in North America come from what is now Québec and date back to 1766. The story goes that residents living in the area around what is now Québec City were terrorized by werewolf sightings and attacks. On July 21, 1766, the *Québec Gazette* claimed that a werewolf had been appearing to people in the form of a beggar. The beast walked on its two hind legs and was "as dangerous as that which appear'd last year in the Country of Gevaudan." Clearly the *loup-garou* was already well established in area folklore. Various newspaper accounts of werewolf attacks appeared in 1766 and 1767, warning people to "Beware then of the Wiles of this malicious Beast, and take good Care of falling into its Claws."

Were sightings of the *loup-garou* a simple case of mistaken identity, and the werewolf nothing more than a vicious animal rising up on its hind legs? Or does the *loup-garou* still wander Québec's forests, waiting for an unsuspecting target to happen along to provide it with its Sunday dinner?

Unidentified Remains?

Tucked away in the backroom of the world-famous Banff Indian Trading Post are the petrified remains of a creature that has captivated the imagination of visitors for decades.

The remains might also be the one firm piece of evidence that supports the existence of at least one of this country's lake monsters.

The Trading Post, well known for its sale of First Nations' crafts and other local artifacts since the early 1900s, is perhaps Banff's oldest gift shop. The shop was first opened in Morley under the name Sign of the Goat Curio Shop. It was moved to Banff's townsite by its founder, Norman Luxton, not long after it opened for business. Luxton had a keen interest in the local First Nations culture and was eventually named Chief White Shield, honorary chief of the Stoney Nakoda First Nation.

Luxton was well known in the Banff community, having established other founding businesses including Banff's newspaper, the *Crag and Canyon*, the Lux Theatre and the King Edward Hotel. And in 1915, Luxton added yet another contribution to the community. He allegedly purchased (or caught at nearby Lake Minnewanka, depending on the story you choose to believe) and permanently displayed, a merman.

At 28 kilometres long, and measuring depths of up to 142 metres, Lake Minnewanka has offered anglers an abundance of lake trout, Rocky Mountain whitefish and several other species. But according to the Stoney Nakoda people, the kind of fish you fillet and serve for dinner aren't the only species living in Minnewanka's deep waters. Their legends describe a monster of demonic proportions that inhabits the lake, scanning the surface and claiming any human victim boating or fishing nearby. In fact, the half-man/half-fish creature, said to have long sharp claws and webbed fingers, the head of a man, a scaled body and the tail of a fish, so craved human flesh that the Stoney originally named the lake M'ne-sto or Cannibal Lake.

One historical eyewitness, purportedly the first person to ever see the lake, allegedly noticed some kind of frightening water creature from a nearby mountain peak and described it as stretching "the length of the lake." The story led to the lake's nickname, "Lake of the Evil Water Spirit." And since Cannibal Lake was such a negative name and would do nothing to attract visitors or trade to the area, it was renamed Minnee-wah-kah in 1888. Translated from the original Stoney, *minnee-wah-kah* means "lake of the water spirit."

Is it possible Luxton really captured a lake spirit? If so, his merman was certainly a lot smaller than the giant fish of the above-mentioned eyewitness account. And if Luxton did actually capture the merman, the Stoney people, who traditionally stayed clear of the lake and believed the water demon would die only if it was struck by lightning, would have certainly hailed him as a hero.

It is also possible that Luxton purchased the merman, as some sources suggest, in an effort to support the Native legend with proof that such a creature did exist—stories of the existence of such a creature date back to early Greek mythology. Apparently Luxton did have a bill of sale for "one fish-man," which he displayed, along with his mummified skeleton, at its unveiling.

Yet another suggestion, though admittedly deflating, is possible. Luxton could have built the creature himself using nothing more than remnants from animal carcasses and some form of papier-mâché technique to popularize the Stoney legend and build interest in the area, his curio shop and the boat tours he operated on Minnewanka.

There are likely as many theories about the origin of Banff's merman as there are visitors to the trading post. Cryptozoologists no doubt support the theory that the merman is authentic. There are reported sightings of mermen in other locations around the world, and the Discovery Channel has even run documentaries on the subject. But to date no official scientific studies have been conducted on the remains, leaving the origins of Banff's infamous merman a mystery that will continue to baffle visitors.

DID YOU KNOW?

The merman isn't Lake Minnewanka's only strange resident. Since 1895, stories of the Lake Minnewanka Wildman have circulated among explorers, trappers and prospectors alike. The Wildman was reported to be more than 2 metres tall after one trapper noticed a large creature ducking a tree limb as it was running into the woods. When the trapper inspected the broken limb, he noted it was more than 2 metres above the ground, giving the man a general idea of the creature's height. The Wildman was spotted several times each year between its initial sighting and its last, in the early winter of 1899, when it was spotted limping in the distance. Some have suggested the Wildman had been injured by gunshot wounds so many times it either decided to take up residence in a more remote location or died of its injuries.

Big Foot Visits Small Town

The hamlet of Seven Persons, Alberta, listed a population of 270 in the 2011 Census, and 231 of those individuals reside in the actual community of Seven Persons. Cyril Ogston founded the settlement in the late 19th century. As a practicing Mormon and polygamist, Ogston was one of many Mormons who left the United States for Canada following a 1862 decision by the U.S. Congress to make polygamy illegal in that country. And although the community attracted other Mormons looking for the freedom to practice their religion as they saw fit, the settlement's population remained small. So when one and then another resident reported a strange occurrence of any kind, it was taken seriously.

It was a report by two young boys made in the fall of 1972 that got local rancher Leonard Edvarson's interest up. The boys said they were walking near a place called Police Point when they noticed a strange animal-like creature walking ahead of them. It was large like a bear, but walking upright, like a human. Startled, the boys told anyone who would listen about what they saw. No one really believed them except, perhaps, Edvarson.

It wasn't until December 1973 that another report started circulating in the Seven Persons area. A man allegedly saw a strange creature wandering about the community streets at about 3:00 AM. It was a bright, moonlit night, giving the witness a clear view of what appeared to be a large being, measuring more than 2 metres tall. The creature looked to be maimed or injured, either missing one of its forearms or holding it pulled tightly against its chest. The next day, strange tracks measuring 38 centimetres long, and 17.8 centimetres wide, with a stride of about 1.8 metres were noticed along the nearby creek bed. Two men fishing discovered similar tracks on the Murray Dam.

One sighting by a couple of boys could be a hoax. A second sighting by another, independent source probably caused tongues to wag. But when the strange footprints appeared, the people of Seven Persons may have started to worry. Edvarson was documenting the sightings and strange accounts, and more came forth. On hearing about the sighting in Seven Persons, another farmer reported that something spooked his cattle so much that they broke out of their corrals.

Other residents saw strange things as well. Edvarson received at least two letters from someone signed "An Observer." The first of those letters described a sighting in nearby Medicine Hat. The witness said he thought at first that he saw a bear, but it was walking upright, albeit with an awkward gait, and looked to be carrying something. According to the letter, the creature went into the creek and disappeared into the bushes. The witness didn't put much stock in what he saw and thought it might have simply been a Halloween joke. But Edvarson must have written a letter in the local newspaper, and when the Observer noticed it, he started thinking about what he'd seen. He decided to sketch what he remembered and wrote to Edvarson, offering to make copies of his sketches. He did not provide Edvarson with his identity—he didn't want people calling him—but that didn't stop him from contacting Edvarson again.

Edvarson received a second letter, along with two sketches of the unknown creature, a few days later. In this letter the writer describes what he saw in greater detail. The creature had short, thick legs, reddish brown fur and was walking "sideways at a very odd gait." The writer again suggested it could be an "early Halloween 'spook,'" but he also noticed a flaw in his theory: "…why would the figure have entered the cold creek? Wouldn't that have been carried too far by some jokester?"

The writer also noted there were no other witnesses, so it wasn't like a jokester was putting on a show for a crowd. Still, the Observer remained reluctant to sign his name and suggested he wouldn't bother Edvarson again, adding his story shouldn't be made public.

These strange accounts collectively represent the sum total of the reported sightings of the unusual creature seen in and around the Seven Persons area. If it was a sasquatch, as some have suggested, perhaps it moved on to a more wooded, remote area more typical of Big Foot habitat. If the whole thing was a hoax, it was never revealed or, at least, never made public.

The sightings have been called "one of the most well known of all Alberta [sasquatch] reports." What these witnesses actually saw remains a mystery.

A WALK ON THE WILD SIDE

BELIEFS, BEHAVIOURS AND ANCIENT LEGENDS

Woman of the Sea

This weird creature of the water achieved legendary status among Canada's Inuit people, but it's unclear if any eyewitnesses ever verified its existence. In this legend, two giants (one version of this tale suggests they were both male giants) lived together alongside the Inuit. Although they were of great stature, they posed no threat to their human cohabitants.

That all changed when one of the giants became pregnant and had a baby daughter. (In the version of the story where both giants were male, the pregnant partner's penis splits in half, and he becomes a woman to give birth.) The daughter had a voracious appetite, even gnawing on her parents' arms. The giants were so disturbed by their daughter's behaviour that they decided to sacrifice her to the sea. Of course, a girl that tried to eat her parents' arms didn't go quietly. She clung to the boat with such determination that eventually her parents had to cut off all her fingers and toes. As the digits fell into the water, they transformed into whales, seals and other sea creatures. With their daughter now cast into the sea, the frightened giants paddled back to shore.

That discarded girl became known as Sedna, Great Mother of sea creatures. To this day, she guards the sea.

Going Wendigo

Far more frightening even than the *loup-garou* is the First Nations' account of the Wendigo. Other monster legends sometimes display a gentler side of a creature, but the Wendigo has no redeeming qualities.

Some witnesses unfortunate enough to catch a glimpse of the Wendigo described it as extremely tall, towering over the tallest man. The creature's ashen skin was stretched tightly across its bony limbs, its eyes were sunken deep in its sockets and its jagged teeth and tattered lips were bloody from the meal of its last victim. It smelled of death. Other accounts describe the monster as hairy with long claws. Still others suggest it was deformed in some way.

What all accounts agree on is just how vicious the Wendigo can be. Its first thought on spying its prey is to attack and consume. Some say that feasting on the flesh of humans makes the Wendigo grow larger and, consequently, more ravenous. Other stories suggest that certain death is perhaps the least frightening threat a Wendigo poses; possessing its victims and driving them to murder is far more disturbing. Northern Alberta Native Swift Runner claimed the spirit of Wendigo took over his body during the cold winter months of 1878 and instructed him to murder and consume his entire family. It was said that Swift Runner had "gone Wendigo."

Stories of the Wendigo occupy the folklore of many of North America's Aboriginal peoples. In Canada, these stories were particularly popular among the Anishinaabe, Ojibwe and Cree peoples. The threat of Wendigo was so feared that village shaman would regularly counsel people on the subject. Jack Fiddler, also known as Zhauwuno-geezhigo-gaubow or "He who stands in the southern sky," was born in 1839 and served as chief and shaman among the Sucker clan of the Anishinaabe in what is now northwestern Ontario. Fiddler claimed fighting the Wendigo kept him very busy; he said he'd killed 14 during his 68 years. Sadly, Jack took his own life after being arrested for the murder of a terminally ill family member. As was the custom of their people, both Jack and his brother Joseph were responsible for euthanizing the sick in an effort to prevent someone from "going Wendigo." After Jack's death, Joseph proceeded to trial and was convicted and sentenced to death.

It has been argued that people who were said to have gone Wendigo actually suffered from a mental illness known as Wendigo psychosis. Typically, people with this condition suffer from nausea and vomiting, and a strange and insatiable craving for human flesh.

Did the vicious monster known as Wendigo prowl Canada's uninhabited wilds? Does the creature still exist, waiting for an unsuspecting victim to wander by? Or was the crazed desire for human flesh, as experienced by Swift Runner, a strange and tragic mental illness.

Chances are we will never be sure.

A Giant of a Tale

Here's another story for the fact or fiction file. While scanning the Internet, I came across an article allegedly printed in the *West Coast Times,* Issue 1924, dated November 29, 1871 entitled "Lost City of Giants Discovered in Toronto, Canada." The story told of how three men, Reverend Nathaniel Wardell, Orin Wardell and Daniel Fredenburg discovered a mass grave containing the remains of some 200 people while digging on Fredenburg's farm, located along the Grand River in Cayuga township. The skeletons were huge, most measuring between 2 and 2.7 metres long. Although they were well preserved, it was clear by their "broken and dented" skulls that these unfortunate individuals met with a violent death.

Assorted personal items were also discovered in the grave, including large stone pipes that were posed in the jaws of some of the skeletons. And despite the fact that there didn't appear to be any children buried there, it was initially believed that the discovery represented a civilization that met with its demise centuries before the farmland where they were unearthed had been cleared of its trees.

Wanting to share his discovery with his neighbours, Fredenburg left the pit open for some time, allowing locals to view the site. But when skulls and bones started disappearing, he filled in the grave. Today, all that remains of Fredenburg's discovery is the old journal story and its reprints in other newspapers of the day.

Of course, someone cared enough to dig up the story and put it on the Internet. In fact, the story of this burial site of giants pops up in several websites dedicated to unravelling the mystery behind this and other similar discoveries of giant-sized skeletons throughout North America.

Did a race of giants once roam this continent, or the world for that matter, as some researchers believe and various ancient religious texts suggest? Could these skeletons represent visitors from another planet? Or are stories of this nature nothing more than urban legends, as international rumour debunker Snopes.com suggests of the claims of giant skeleton discoveries that have been circulating the Internet in the last decade?

I'll leave that for you to decide.

ANIMAL ODDITIES

FURS, FINS AND FEATHERS

It is wonderful to feel the grandness of Canada in the raw, not because she is Canada but because she's something sublime that you were born into, some great rugged power that you are a part of.

–Emily Carr

In the grand scheme of things, it wasn't that long ago that Canada was an untamed wilderness. Fly over British Columbia and it's easy to see there are still vast expanses of wilderness. At the same time, towns and cities continue to expand, and the family farm grows into big business requiring more and more land. So where do all our wild critters go? Some of them, as you'll see, like to hang out with us bipedal creatures. Others just like to pass through from time to time. Still others need us to give them a helping hand.

DID YOU  KNOW?

Canada is a polar bear haven, with almost 60 percent of the world's cold-weather beauties living in this country.

Polar Bear Capital

Churchill likes to call itself the polar bear capital of the world because of the large number of polar bears that wander inland every fall, but that distinction comes with a few difficulties. For example, these bears don't understand that their territory doesn't include the town of Churchill itself, and they tend to roam about at will. A confrontation with one of these massive creatures could spell disaster for the human population. So as an added safety measure, folks living in Churchill leave their car doors unlocked as a courtesy to their fellow townsfolk. That way, should a bear suddenly decide to saunter down Main Street, pedestrians can quickly dash into the nearest vehicle.

Wildlife Traffic Lanes

Ontario built its first animal-only traffic bridge in 2012. The Ministry of Transportation built the multi-million dollar project, located south of Sudbury, over Highway 69 near the Killarney turn-off, in an effort to protect area wildlife from crossing a particularly high-traffic stretch of road. It is hoped that the 6 kilometres of fencing on either side of the highway will re-direct the moose and other wildlife to pass safely over the bridge.

The construction cost the Ontario government a ton of cash, but the first-of-its-kind structure in the province pales in comparison to Alberta's efforts at granting its wildlife safe passage. This province boasts 38 underpasses and six overpasses, located throughout Banff National Park and stretching as far southeast to British Columbia's Yoho National Park. All are dedicated to providing safe passage for bears, wolves, lynx and the like.

DID YOU  KNOW?

Alberta's Wood Buffalo National Park, created in 1922, was built to protect the largest concentration of wood bison in the world. The park also provides the "nesting habitat of the last remaining wild migratory flock of whooping cranes." In 1941, there were only about 21 birds, but with efforts of the Committee on the Status of Endangered Wildlife that population has recovered to some degree. One estimate from December 2010 suggests the Wood Buffalo flock is about 263 strong and the world population sits at about 568. The increase in numbers is heartening but not enough to take the whooping crane off the endangered species list.

Fatty Fish

The topic of water pollution aside, many nutritionists still consider fish one of the best foods for a healthy diet. One reason for the commendation is that fish is typically a lean source of protein.

Of course there's an exception to every rule.

The oolichan is a small smelt that looks like an oversized sardine. Most adults measure between 15 and 20 centimetres, roughly the length of the average adult hand, but some have reached lengths of 30 centimetres. And while the oolichan continue to be an important part of the diet of First Nations peoples living along the Pacific Coast, food isn't the only thing they're used for. What makes this species particularly unique is they are a very fatty fish—as much as 15 percent of their small bodies is fat. Traditionally, Canada's Indigenous peoples as well as early explorers would dry the oolichan and burn them like candles, hence this fish's other common name, "candlefish."

Bewildering Fish Story

Alberta is home to 65 species of fish, 54 of which are native to the province. The bull trout is Alberta's provincial fish and by most accounts is plentiful in many of the province's lakes and rivers. The thing is, the bull trout likes its food. It gobbles up other fish, crustaceans and mollusks on lake and river bottoms, as well as the insects it sees on the water's surface.

But the bull trout prefers calmer waters; it doesn't like the constant strain of swimming against the current. So why, then, is the bull trout the only species of fish to establish itself in the turbulent waters at the top of Athabasca Falls? And how did it get there? Even if it had the determination of a salmon, there's no way it leapt the 23 metres from the bottom of the falls to the top. And if such a feat were even possible, what would have been its motivation? The 14 species of native fish that live at the base of the falls seem to be quite content there.

Mysteries demand theories, some of which are infinitely more plausible than others. Ward Hughson, Jasper National Park Aquatics Specialist, suggests that the bull trout made their way to the head of the falls via ice dams formed during the glacial evolution of the valley. That might explain how a fish could have established itself at the top of Athabasca Falls, but it certainly doesn't explain why the bull trout is the only fish to have done so. The bull trout inhabits the head of other waterfalls, but in those cases it cohabits with other fish species. As the only fish species to inhabit the waters at the top of the Athabasca Falls, the bull trout's food supply is limited.

Is it possible that early explorers to the area introduced the bull trout to the head of Athabasca Falls? Or could it be that a bird of prey dropped the first unsuspecting fish there, as Blair Yersz of Bow River Adventures suggests?

Tyhee Lake Mystery Fish

Tyhee Lake, located in British Columbia's beautiful Bulkley Valley, is home to at least one fish mystery. Aside from providing anglers with a one-of-a-kind story to tell when they go home, and keeping British Columbia's conservationists busy studying and protecting the species, not much is known about the giant pygmy whitefish. In fact, there has been some debate about whether there is such a species or if the pygmy whitefish caught in this small northern lake is just a really well fed whitefish. In any case, there are only two locations in British Columbia where this particular fish is located—in the Bulkley Valley's Tyhee Lake and the Caribou country's McLeese Lake, located between Williams Lake and Quesnel. The fish are currently listed on BC's official "red list," a government list that names and protects all species that are endangered or threatened in the province.

DID YOU KNOW?

Canada boasts a mind-boggling 200,000 kilometres of coastline and more than seven million square kilometres of territorial waters. It's little wonder that our country is a leader in marine research, and the mysteries of ocean life are something scientists are just beginning to decipher. According to one estimate, about one million marine species exist. Of that number, scientists at the World Register of Marine Species have catalogued 226,000 and have another 72,000 in the queue for detailed investigation. That leaves an amazing 700,000 more marine species to collect and study. Some of those species are unique to Canadian waters; at this point it's believed that one species of sea pen lives exclusively in the Gulf of St. Lawrence.

Strange Claim to Fame

Manitoba has a unique claim to fame that might make most people's skin crawl. The hamlet of Narcisse is one of 11 small communities that make up the rural municipality of Armstrong. The 2011 census posted a total human population of 1835 for all of Armstrong, and the human inhabitants in the area are far outnumbered by the red-sided garter snakes.

The Wildlife Branch of Manitoba Conservation estimates more than fifty thousand snakes make their home in and around the Narcisse Snake Dens, located just outside the community of Narcisse. Observation decks dot the 3 kilometres of self-guided interpretive trail provided for visitors to learn more about the snakes and their habitat without causing them or their environment any harm.

Red-sided garter snakes can be found from the Northwest Territories south to Oklahoma. Their habitat in Canada stretches from Ontario to British Columbia. These snakes prefer to live near ponds where they can feed on frogs, leeches and the like, and hide away from their natural predators. While there are no doubt countless prime habitats within the area these snakes are found, this Manitoba tourist destination is internationally known for having the largest concentration of snakes in the world. It also has a giant snake as a roadside attraction to let travellers know of its claim to fame.

Cat Lovers Legacy

Beauty is most definitely in the eye of the beholder when it comes to the Canadian Sphynx. A hairless kitten aptly named Prune was born to cat lovers in Roncesvalles, a neighbourhood in Toronto, in 1966. The owners were intrigued, and the kitten was later bred with its mother in the hope of producing another hairless offspring. The breeding was successful and captured the interest of a science graduate named Ridyadh Bawa, who further explored the recessive gene responsible for the anomaly. Today, the Canadian Sphynx is an established breed. If you ask me, the young kittens look a little like Yoda of *Star Wars* fame.

ANIMAL ODDITIES

Birds of a Feather

In the 1880s, a group of forward-thinking settlers living in the area of Last Mountain and Long Lake lobbied what was then known as the Dominion of Canada to set aside a large parcel of land in what, 18 years later, would become the province of Saskatchewan. These settlers were concerned for the waterfowl that frequented the area, and they didn't want their breeding grounds destroyed or diminished by the development of the Qu'Appell-Long Lake-Saskatoon Railway.

Their concerns were considered, and John A. MacDonald, prime minister at the time, set aside 1000 hectares as the Last Mountain Lake Bird Sanctuary, making it the first designated bird sanctuary in North America. Today this sanctuary, which has grown to more than 15,600 hectares, provides home, stopover and breeding locations for more than 280 bird species, several of which are considered vulnerable, threatened or endangered.

Oh, Rats!

The Norway rat isn't something you're happy to find on your property. In fact, Alberta Agriculture calls it "one of the most destructive creatures known to man." So if you are looking for a foolproof way of avoiding rats altogether, you may want to consider moving to Alberta. The province was historically the only place in the world where you won't find the pesky Norway rat. That said, a report in 2012 raised considerable concern when an 80-metre-long rat nest was discovered in a Medicine Hat landfill. According to a Global news report, it took 21 workers and two excavators about six hours to eliminate the nest, leaving Alberta's rat-free status, at least in the southeastern corner of the province, shattered.

Still, Alberta's "rat patrol" is on full alert at all times to ensure this disturbing find remains an anomaly.

Not All Honks Are Alike

Canada geese are remarkable creatures. Whether they are returning from a winter in more balmy climes or heading south before the bite of the Canadian cold gets too harsh, the V-formation they travel in makes them impossible to miss. Then there's that honk—wait a minute, I mean those calls. While their "honk" is what most of us connect with Canada geese, it is not the only call they make. They actually use other sounds as well when communicating with each other. Researchers speculate the Canada goose has as many as 13 unique calls for, according to Ducks Unlimited, "things like greetings, warnings and contentment." In fact, scientists suggest that they "may be one of the most talkative animals after humans."

DID YOU KNOW?

Not all Canada geese are created equal. Scientists generally agree that there are 11 different races of Canada geese. Although they share many characteristics, like their long black necks and body colour, they differ in size and wingspan.

Beaver Mansion

And now for a Google Earth discovery of another kind. Researchers using satellite imagery first spotted the mother of all beaver dams in Wood Buffalo National Park, almost 200 kilometres northeast of Fort McMurray in 2007. Estimates put the dam at a 850 metres long, and based on the assortment of vegetation growing on top, the structure has been under construction for generations of beaver families. Researchers may have been interested in getting a closer look at the behemoth creation, but the structure was so remote that it was thought to be inaccessible.

Enter New Jersey explorer Rob Mark. With treks on his record that include such exotic locations as the Amazon, Mark believed he was up to the task. Equipped with as much information as he could gather, the explorer boated to the shores of Lac Clair. From there he started out on the toughest 16-kilometre hike he'd ever taken. Ploughing through dense, mosquito-infested bush and swampy muskeg earned him the title of the first man known to have visited the dam, though historically First Nations hunters would have no doubt passed through the area.

New Kind of Zoo
A trip to West Edmonton Mall offers patrons countless shopping and entertainment options, including a peek at several animal species. In fact, the mall is not just a shopping Mecca; it's a zoo that's accredited by the Canadian Association of Zoos and Aquariums (CAZA).

That's Awkward
Staying put doesn't guarantee trouble won't find you. Such was the case for six young squirrels sharing nest by a pine tree near Regina, Saskatchewan. While they were resting, the tree's sap dripped on their tails and essentially superglued them together. The squirrels were caught and taken to a local vet clinic where workers sedated them and unravelled the mess. Vets call the situation "squirrel kings," and warn that it can be potentially deadly because the squirrels can't feed as well as usual, and the tangled tails can become raw and infected. The squirrels in this story were successfully disentangled and their tails healed.

Canada's Own White Walkers
The Kermode bear of the central and northern portion of Canada's Pacific Northwest is also known as the spirit or ghost bear, and there's a good reason for that. They're as white as a ghost, for one thing. Their eyes have an ethereal quality about them, especially in the dark. And if you watch closely, it almost looks as if they're suspended, just an inch or two above the ground, as they walk. I know. I watched one close up, just a thin wall of wood separating us.

The fact is the Kermode bear is, physiologically speaking, really a black bear. It was news to me, too, when I first heard it. A Kermode has white fur, instead of the traditional black, because both of its parents would have carried a recessive gene. Like all black bears, the Kermode still has a dark nose and paws.

The Kermode got its name from Francis Kermode, the provincial museum worker credited with its discovery. But the really weird thing about the Kermode is that you won't find one anywhere else in Canada—or anywhere else in the world—outside of the specific area of BC, stretching from the Burke Channel to the Nass River, as well as the Princess Royal and Gribbell islands. It leaves one to wonder why black bears with this recessive gene only live in this part of the country?

A Whale of a Find

Farmers in south-central Manitoba know about tilling fields, growing crops like corn and sunflowers and raising livestock. But when a farmer came across some weirdly shaped bones back in 1974, he scratched his head in wonder. What was eventually unearthed was the fossil of a 13-metre long mosasaur, Tylosaurus pembinensis—a marine reptile believed to have lived at least 80 million years ago. The Manitoba find made the record books as being the largest mosasaur discovered to date.

More than 40 years later, on November 26, 2014, Cameron Friesen, Tory MLA for the Morden-Winkler region, put forth a private member's bill suggesting Bruce, (as the reconstructed reptile is fondly referred to by staff at the Canadian Fossil Discovery Centre in Morden), be recognized as Manitoba's official marine reptile fossil emblem.

ANIMAL ODDITIES

WILDLIFE MYSTERIES

A Death of Another Feather

The odd dead bird might not raise a lot of concern, but when Leona Green of the Hillspring Wildlife Rehabilitation Centre in Dawson Creek noticed ravens and crows dropping like flies in the summer of 2013, she decided to investigate.

Green told *Canadian Geographic* that although no one knows why, more than 30 ravens and crows were discovered paralyzed, and all later died. At least six of the birds were sent to provincial labs to be tested for West Nile virus, but all tested negative. While that doesn't definitively rule out the disease in the remaining 20-something cases, the negative test results, coupled with the fact that British Columbia's West Nile Virus surveillance program has not discovered a single bird or human case since 2010, makes it unlikely.

Did these avian victims succumb to pesticides or pollutants? Could have they been exposed to a form of avian botulism? Or was it merely coincidence that so many birds died in exactly the same way?

Tainted Waters?

Between April and May in 2013, Ontario Parks ecologists Anna Sheppard and Ed Mooris discovered 59 dead turtles along the shores of Misery Bay Provincial Park, on Manitoulin Island. Forty-nine of those were Blandings turtles, and the other 10 were painted turtles.

The two scientists were studying the turtles' migrations, habits and habitat at the time of their disturbing find. Since that time, several other ecologists have used their expertise to try and determine why turtles in this location are dying in such large numbers. At this point ranavirus, an infections disease that's been attributed to amphibian deaths elsewhere, has been ruled out. Researchers also don't believe the turtles were killed by natural predators.

According to officials from Ontario Parks, protecting the Blandings turtle is of utmost importance because it's considered an umbrella species, meaning that by protecting them you are also protecting other species that live in the same habitat. If researchers can't pinpoint why the turtles are dying, there is no telling what might happen to the rest of the species at Misery Bay.

UNIQUE LAND FORMATIONS

PINGOS, WATER SPOTS AND OTHER ANOMALIES

Canada is so big as to seem invisible.

–Brian Moore

Canada is a huge country with a varied geography that includes boreal forests and Rocky Mountains, Appalachian Mountains and vast prairies, countless lakes and amazing caves for spelunkers to explore. We've even got deserts here! And tucked away within many of these features are gems that will have you scratching your head in wonder.

Reverse Gravity?

Imagine this: you're sitting in your car, it's in neutral, and suddenly you begin rolling backwards and uphill! Strange as it might sound, the mysterious phenomenon is not the figment of an overactive imagination. Or is it?

Magnetic Hill, New Brunswick, is home to one of Canada's most famous gravity hills. Its discovery dates back to the 1880s, when travellers would share tales about a road where wagons would run into a horse's heels even though they were travelling uphill! Stories about the phenomenon continued into the 1930s, and eventually included cars rolling uphill without any help from their motors.

In August 1933, three reporters from the *Saint John Telegraph Journal* decided to investigate the anomaly for themselves. For five hours the trio traversed the back roads, and just when they were about to give up, they decided to stop their car and stretch their legs. That's when their car started to roll uphill! The reporters had brought along various scientific devices to assess what caused the irregularity, but when they noticed water also trickled uphill, they concluded that magnetic pull could not be responsible. Their best guess for the apparent reverse gravity, an optical illusion.

It appears the journalists were on to something.

The best-accepted theory for these so-called gravity hills is that it only looks like something is rolling uphill. It's all an illusion. A view of the horizon could be obstructed. Few or no trees in sight give the viewer less to go on. Visual cues prove deceiving.

Of course, this is all theory too, some might argue. For the residents of Moncton, New Brunswick, their much-loved Magnetic Hill remains a mystery that has tantalized generations and attracted visitors for more than 100 years.

DID YOU KNOW?

Many Canadians know about Moncton's Magnetic Hill, but there are at least nine other lesser-known gravity hills in Canada. British Columbia boasts two: one in Abbotsford, on McKee Road and another in Vernon, on Dixon Dam Road. There is another one in Bridgetown, Nova Scotia, on Hampton Mountain Road north of Valleyview Provincial Park. Four are located in Ontario: on King Road in Burlington, on Escarpment Sideroad near Caledon, on Highway 41 in Dacre and on Ritson Road North in Oshawa. And Québec has two such hills: one also going by the name Magnetic Hill in Chartierville and the other on Route Saint-Louis in Notre-Dame-Auxiliatrice-de-Buckland.

Speaking of Gravity…

Were you aware that parts of Canada, especially the land around Hudson Bay, are missing gravity? Seriously! Parts of our country have less gravity than the rest of the world. This phenomenon was first recorded during the 1960s when gravity fields were being charted around the world, leaving scientists baffled. More than 50 years of research have resulted in two main theories.

First, it was suggested that a process known as convection, which takes place in the molten mass of the Earth's mantle, could have shifted some of the Earth's continental plates, thereby decreasing the mass of a particular area and, coincidentally, decreasing the gravity there as well.

A second theory posits that the Laurentide ice sheet that covered much of North America was thicker and heavier in these areas of missing gravity, playing with the earth's mass and its ability to "bounce back" fully. Again, less mass means less gravity. Of course it's a lot more complicated than these few sentences suggest, and an overall mind-boggling thought altogether!

Spotted Lake

Now you see it; now you don't. South of Osoyoos, British Columbia, is a lake the First Nations call Ktlil'x, more commonly known as Spotted Lake. There are times of the year when the lake looks like most others. But during the summer, the water evaporates, leaving large colourful spots—spots that change colour throughout the summer—to dot the ground.

For centuries, this lake posed a mystery to all who saw it. The First Nations people considered it a sacred site, and although they may not have had the language to describe what occurred there in scientific terms, they knew it was special and believed that the waters had healing properties. According to the Okanagan Valley guide, those properties were so revered that during times of conflict, rival tribes made temporary truces so their wounded warriors could visit the lake.

In time science explained the natural phenomena, calling Spotted Lake a "saline endorheic alkali lake." Simply put, there is a high concentration of about 11 different minerals like magnesium, calcium and sodium sulphates, and the chemical elements of silver and titanium, that are responsible for the colourful deposits in spots of varying size left behind when the water evaporates in the heat of summer. Those minerals are also responsible for its reputation as a lake of healing waters.

Even before the lake evaporates, spots can be seen on the surface as the sun crystallizes the salts in the water, forming hardened, shiny but transparent patches that float. These circular patches form walkways through the lakebed until they eventually sink and become the colourful areas seen once the water is gone. As the mineral concentration changes in the earth, the colours of the spots also change.

Today, Spotted Lake is privately owned by the Okanagan Nation. Its waters are still believed to have mystical qualities that, many believe, defy scientific explanation, no matter how complex. In the words of the Syilx Okanagan Nation Alliance, "Its medicinal powers are not to be taken lightly. This lake is a Chief among lakes, its powers are above the purely physical. It contains 365 circles in various shapes, sizes and depths. Each particular day of the year. Anyone who goes to this lake will find the right circle if he seeks."

DID YOU  KNOW?

Some of the minerals at Spotted Lake were used to manufacture ammunition during World War I.

Healing Waters

My mother first told me about Manitou Beach, a salt-water lake near Watrous, Saskatchewan. She said that's where she learned to swim. She thought she was a very good swimmer indeed, until she tried to swim in fresh water and sank. It's a well-known fact that salt water helps buoy up swimmers, but there's a lot more to water at Lake Manitou—it is alleged to have healing properties.

Are you in need of hair tonic, toothpaste, a salve for sore muscles? Various minerals, oils and other properties derived from the waters of Lake Manitou, in particular the magnesium sulphate and iron oxide contained therein, have been used in the making of these and many other health products. In fact, it's believed that these waters have the highest mineral content of any lake in North America. The waters have been compared to the famous spa city of Carlsbad, in the Czech Republic, earning Lake Manitou the nickname "Carlsbad of Canada."

As with most of Canada's natural wonders, it was First Nations people who discovered the lake and its healing properties, although it appears to have happened quite by accident. Legend has it that Native peoples trying to escape a small pox epidemic in 1837 happened upon the lake. Two young men in the group were particularly ill and were left in a tent on the shores of Lake Manitou. Once the rest of their party continued on, the men inched their way into the water, looking to soothe their wounds and cool their fevered bodies. After a few days the men found they'd regained their strength, their fever broke and they were able to rejoin their party. From that time on, these waters were called Lake Manitou because they believed the lake's healing qualities came from the Great Spirit or Manitou.

On early summer mornings, a thick mist often hangs over the waters of Lake Manitou, giving it a mystique that only adds to its allure. The mysterious healing powers at Lake Manitou may defy a complete scientific explanation, but for the many visitors who travel great distances to swim in its silky waters or enjoy a healing massage in one of the many businesses offering a variety of holistic health opportunities, they are very real. Over the years visitors have claimed the waters eased the pain of their arthritis, or healed it outright, cleared up eczema and sped up the healing of open wounds.

DID YOU KNOW?

Shrimp and other crustaceans grow in salt water, so it should be no surprise that brine shrimp can be found in the waters of Lake Manitou. In the early 1960s, a man named Frank Debevc harvested, processed and sold the tiny shrimp found there to pet food stores. The tiny creatures measured just 85 millimetres when fully grown.

Pingos, You Say?

We might not have the highest pingo, but Canada is home to the largest concentration of this unique landscape formation in the world. Simply put, pingos are land heaves that look a little like mini volcanoes, only instead of having lava at their core, their foundation is ice. They occur in areas of the world where freeze and thaw cycles cause changes to the landscape. Canada's arctic region is prime real estate for pingos to form, which is why we have more pingos than anywhere else in the world. Parks Canada estimates there are about 1350 pingos near the community of Tuktoyaktuk in the Northwest Territories. Our highest pingo is Ibyuk, rising 49 metres from its base and measuring about 300 metres in diameter. The only pingo that is larger is Kadleroshilik, located near Prudhoe Bay, Alaska. It measures 54 metres high.

Living Sand

Driving through Saskatchewan along the Trans Canada Highway has no doubt led to the perspective so many Canadians have of the province's landscape—namely that the most exciting scenery you see are the fence posts lining the ditches. Granted this stretch of Saskatchewan is flatter than many other provinces, but it's far from an accurate representation of the whole. Saskatchewan is home to a wide assortment of natural wonders, one of which has garnered international recognition.

Tucked away in the boreal forest region that makes up the majority of northern Saskatchewan are the Lake Athabasca Sand Dunes. This unique land feature snakes along about 100 kilometres of the lake's south shore and is considered the "largest active sand surface in Canada and one of the most northern sets of major dune fields in the world." These dunes, thought to have formed about 8000 years ago at the end of the last ice age, shift and move with the wind and water, creating an unstable and ever-changing topography that is stunning to look at.

Along with its amazing beauty, this unique and fragile area is home to 10 plant species found nowhere else in the world! Some of these endemic species are:

- felt-leaved willow *(Salix silicicola),*
- Tyrrell's willow *(Salix planifolia tyrrellii),*
- inland sea thrift *(Armeria maritima),*
- field chickweed *(Cerastium arvense),*
- Mackenzie hairgrass *(Deschampsia mackenzieana),*
- floxxose tansy *(Tanacetum huronense* var. *floccosum*), and
- stemless lady's slipper *(Cypripedium acaule).*

Why this flora thrives here and nowhere else remains a scientific mystery.

A Sandy Situation

The sparkling lakes and sandy beaches of Ontario's Sandbanks Provincial Park is a popular summer destination for residents and tourists alike. The park is home to "the largest baymouth bar (a large sand dune that separates one body of water from another) on a freshwater lake in the world." And the sand dunes the area is so popular for can reach as high as 60 metres.

But some of those sand dunes also hold another claim to fame. They ate an entire town!

According to a letter written by Ontario Land and Parks in response to a question posed by a young Raymond Ricketts back in November 1961, a small community was establishing itself in that area toward the end of the 19th century. A brick factory had been build there, along with a road, hotel and a scattering of small homes. In order to establish the town, the land had to be cleared, but removing the trees caused considerable erosion, leaving the sand dunes to inch their way toward the small community and eventually overtake the buildings. By the time residents realized what had happened, any attempt to reforest the area was unsuccessful. The sand had taken over, and the town was buried!

Raymond had originally asked if a tidal wave had caused the sandy dunes to form, and if it had buried anything during its creation. Bet he didn't expect the answer he received!

Sandy Seconds

Saskatchewan boasts a second, but no less marvellous, set of sand dunes. The Great Sand Hills cover about 1900 square kilometres of the southwestern corner of the province. Like their counterpart in the north, these dunes are always remaking themselves, changing design and direction with the ever-changing wind.

DID YOU KNOW?

There are lots of caves in Canada. In fact, there are so many caves in Canada that researchers can't even begin to number them; new caves are being discovered, and even the ones that have been spelunked are far from efficiently explored. Canada's longest cave, at more than 20,000 metres long, is the Castleguard Cave, located in Banff National Park. The Heavy Breather system, located in the Flathead wilderness of southeastern British Columbia, is the deepest Canadian cave discovered to date. It measures 653 metres.

Small Town, Big Surprises?

Tucked away in the southwestern corner of Saskatchewan is the small gem of a town called Eastend, population 527. The quaint main street and neighbouring homes speak of a cozy community offering all the comforts of home.

What isn't immediately obvious is that Eastend offers a selection of fascinating natural marvels. Its location is unique as it is in the Cypress Hills, the wonders of which are maintained and protected by the Saskatchewan and Alberta governments in the form of the Cypress Hills Interprovincial Park. Incidentally, this is the country's only interprovincial park.

Just outside of town is the internationally renowned T.rex Discovery Centre. In 1991 Scotty, the largest, most complete *Tyrannosaurus rex* ever unearthed was discovered in the area. The 65-million-year-old giant, along with the plethora of other ancient finds, is displayed and researched at this world-class facility.

If prehistoric giants aren't enough, there's more. Grab a copy of The Continental Divide road tour pamphlet and jump into your car and you'll find an assortment of natural wonders, beginning with an interesting mound of earth known as Chocolate Peak. The hill got its name after a clay miner tried to burn the coal at its crest. The problem was he couldn't put the fire out, and it continued to smoulder for years, turning the hill the chocolate colour it was named for.

A little farther down the trail, about 24 kilometres from town, is the Dividing Springs Ranch, so named because of a unique, geological feature located there that marks a dividing point for creeks and rivers in the area. According to the pamphlet, tributaries north of that point flow as far away as Hudson Bay, 1808 kilometres northeast of the site. Creeks and rivers south of that point make their way to the Gulf of Mexico, 2768 kilometres south.

Jury Still Out

Genetic mutation or alien implantation? The jury is still out on what is responsible for a strange grove of twisted trees found on a privately owned farm north of Hafford, Saskatchewan. These trees have captured the imagination of residents for generations, largely because they're so vastly different in appearance from the aspens growing a half dozen metres across the road from this particular farm. Apparently, cuttings from these trees have been planted in Manitoba, and the adult versions display the same characteristics as their donors, which has reinforced the idea that a genetic mutation is responsible for these physical oddities. But stretch that thought just a little and consider—what caused these mutations in the first place?

DID YOU  KNOW?

The highest elevation between the Rocky Mountains and Labrador can be found in the Cypress Hills. Their highest elevation is more than 1460 metres.

Alberta's Guardian

Lynn Hickox was searching Google Earth and looking for the most direct route from her Gravelbourg home in Saskatchewan to Drumheller, Alberta, when she discovered an Alberta landmark a little farther south that some believe has a strong link to a Blackfoot legend. The bird's-eye view of land gave Hickox a unique perspective of Alberta's landscape, and as she scanned the area around Medicine Hat, she noticed a formation that looked like the face of a First Nations' chief in full, feathered headdress. Hickox logged her find on Google Earth, stimulating media interest from as far away as Australia. The CBC radio show *As It Happens* even hosted a "Name the Formation" contest and came up with the name Guardian of the Badlands, but in the end the formation was named the Badlands Guardian.

The cause of the image itself isn't much of a mystery. Over time, wind and water eroded the clay-rich soil and, as chance would have it, created what from a distance looks like a chief in headdress. What is mysterious about the formation is that it is located in an area revered by the Blackfoot nation. The legend set in the area is the impetus for the naming of Medicine Hat and ties in coincidentally with the image of the Badlands Guardian.

According to the legend, to save his people from starvation, a young brave of the Blood tribe sacrificed everything to appease water spirits that were believed to inhabit a part of the South Saskatchewan River between Police Point and Strathcona Park. At one point the spirit, in the form of a giant serpent, rose from the water and promised to give the young brave a *saamis*—a headdress made from eagle feathers that the serpent called a "medicine hat." The serpent also gifted the young brave with the abilities of a medicine man. With these powers, the young man could save his people. But it would cost him. The serpent wanted the young brave's wife. Try as he might, the brave couldn't appease the serpent with any other sacrifice, and eventually he handed his wife over to the serpent. The brave donned the hat of eagle feathers and saved his people.

So what of the Badlands Guardian? Is the image of the medicine man carved into the rocky landscape near Medicine Hat a likeness of this hero miraculously preserved as a permanent memorial to his efforts? Or is it just a coincidence that Hickox noticed the nuances of the landscape formed an image that, at another time, in a different light, no one else would recognize?

Immortalized in Stone

An aerial view of the Sleeping Giant of Sleeping Giant Provincial Park, located on Sibley Peninsula near Thunder Bay, Ontario, reveals the image of a peaceful giant. But the legend that turned him into the rock formation the park is known for paints an altogether different picture. According to Ojibwe legend, the Great Spirit Nanabijou (who is known by many names) told an Ojibwe tribe the whereabouts of a silver mine as a gift for their loyalty. There was a condition put on the gift, however; sharing the information with the white men would result in serious consequences. Of course, loose lips prevailed after a night of drinking, and Nanabijou turned into the stone formation we see today.

There are variations of this legend. When I visited the park, I was told a princess also turned to stone, weeping on the chest of the sleeping Nanabijou.

As far as the silver mine is concerned, one was indeed discovered and excavated. Located at the southern tip of the park, at the giant's feet, is Silver Islet, and out into Lake Superior a little ways is a small blip of an island with the same name. This small land mass had the richest silver deposits discovered in the northwest at that time. Silver was actually discovered there in 1845 and was mined until 1883, when water filled the shafts and destroyed any hope of further digging. With the mine gone, the population of the town, Silver Islet, declined. Today, Silver Islet is little more than a summer community, and it's listed on ghosttowns.com as "one of Ontario's best kept ghost towns."

UNIQUE LAND FORMATIONS

Where the Monsters Roamed

Alberta is home to one of the richest locations of dinosaur fossils in the world and to the world-class museums and researchers that support the deposits in the central Alberta town of Drumheller. Dinosaur Provincial Park has produced the skeletons of 40 dinosaur species and more than 500 prehistoric specimens, furnishing many of the world's museums with a glimpse of past life. But why is it that the area known as Alberta's Badlands is so rich with these species?

It's a mystery that has intrigued researchers since the first dinosaur was discovered along the Red Deer River on June 12, 1884. The Royal Tyrrell Museum is named for Joseph Burr Tyrrell, the geologist who discovered the giant. After more than a century of research, a few good theories backed by solid science offer plausible explanations. Royal Tyrrell museum science educator Joanna Northover said that when dinosaurs first roamed Alberta, the land was lush with the vegetation required to support the giant reptiles. And there was water, too. During the mid- to late Cretaceous period, the shallow waters of the Western Interior Seaway covered neighbouring Saskatchewan and into Manitoba.

"At the same time it was a depositional environment, which means more sediments were being deposited than were being eroded," Northover explained, adding that when animals died they were "covered with the sand and mud washing down from the mountains forming to the West...it was a good time to die and become a fossil." Add to that the waters of the Western Interior Seaway blowing in from time to time in the middle of one of the mega-storms, flooding the land and drowning anything in its path, and it makes sense that Alberta was a repository for so many prehistoric remains.

Researchers may have reasoned why the area is a storehouse of fossils and so many other natural wonders, but there is one mystery that won't be answered any time soon—how many additional skeletons will eventually be unearthed, and how many hitherto unknown species will be discovered in Alberta's badlands?

Fairy Chimneys

Perhaps the weirdest looking natural sculptures we can boast about are our famed hoodoos. French explorers were among the first white settlers to come across these natural wonders during travels in the Badlands of Alberta. They called them *chiminees de fee* or "fairy chimneys."

Exactly how these structures earned the name hoodoos is a bit of a mystery. Some scholars suggest European settlers were responsible for the name. Others suggest the word "hoodoo" has a connection to the African American voodoo traditions.

Perhaps even more interesting than the name itself is the Blackfoot legend that the hoodoos were petrified people they called *ma'tapiiks*. The Blackfoot believed *ma'tapiik*s were either "evil spirits trapped in rock; giants that came alive at night to hurl rocks at intruders; or spirits that protected the sacred lands."

PREVAILING CANADIAN MYSTERIES

MISSING BUT PRESUMED DEAD

When we remember we are all mad, the mysteries disappear and life stands explained.

–Mark Twain

People are anything but predictable. And every choice we make unleashes untold consequences, resulting in the stories of our lives weaving together to form the fabric of the communities in which we reside. Most often those consequences connect in a predictable fashion. No mystery involved. But there are times when things don't add up, and the answers to a problem are hidden or non-existent. Here are some of this country's strangest unsolved mysteries.

Missing Village?

It's November 1930 (some sources say 1932, a time of year that's cold just about anywhere in Canada but especially so in the Kivalliq Region of Nunavut. Joe Labelle had spent the better part of the day working his traps and was anxious to turn in for the night. It was getting late, and he was ravenous, so Labelle headed toward an Inuit village at nearby Lake Anjikuni in search of food and a bed for the night.

The problem was, when Labelle arrived, no one was home—not a child, not a grandma, not a dog. The village that was once home to an estimated 30 people was a ghost town.

One building at a time, Labelle searched for any clue as to what happened to cause the villagers to leave. What he discovered confused him even more: pots of caribou stew left uneaten, a child's sealskin coat half-mended, a bone needle still inserted in a garment, a smouldering fire. In addition, it appeared as though pantry shelves were still lined with food, rifles and parkas the villagers would have needed for warmth and protection. None of it made any sense, and despite the sub-zero temperatures, a spooked Labelle high-tailed it from the village to the next safe spot he knew of, a telegraph office located a few kilometres away.

As soon as the Mounties heard Labelle's story, a search party set out for the village. Along the way they stopped by the home of another trapper named Armand Laurent. Laurent told officers that he and his sons noticed a strange object glowing in the night sky. The object morphed from a cylinder into a "bullet-like object" as it crossed the horizon toward the Inuit village. Laurent's story added another layer to Labelle's account, and when the Mounties visited the village, they discovered even more disturbing details. Several of the graves in the frozen ground in the nearby graveyard had been desecrated, the bodies they held removed and stone markers stacked in piles of two—a seemingly impossible feat for that time of year and a taboo in the Inuit culture. The carcasses of several sled dogs were also discovered just outside the village. And while the Mounties were conducting their search, they noticed strange "bluish lights pulsating" over the village.

Accounts of the ghost village and its lost tribe appeared in several newspapers of the day, and in 1959 American writer Frank Edwards included the tale in his book, *Stranger than Science*. The story has been included in several other publications, as well, along with theories on what happened to the villagers living near Lake Anjikuni. Those theories include a mass abduction by an alien species, and an encounter with a demonic spirit or vampires. One writer even speculated the villagers simply disappeared into a parallel reality.

Eventually the RCMP officially disputed the story on their website, suggesting the entire tale is nothing more than an urban legend. "There is no evidence…to support such a story," the website states. "Furthermore, the Mounted Police who patrolled the area recorded no untoward events of any kind and neither did local trappers or missionaries." The denouncement doesn't mention news stories that appeared in newspapers of the day, nor reflect on an RCMP officer named Sergeant J. Nelson who was said to have taken an interest in the story in January 1931 and believed it to be true.

Is the story of the missing Inuit villagers a fabrication? Or did they indeed disappear, earning this location the moniker "Roswell North"?

Actual Event or Urban Legend?

Just about every Canadian over the age of majority, especially if they live west of Ontario, knows of the Banff Springs Hotel. This "castle in the Rockies" was named a national historic site in 1992. Its spectacular architecture is enhanced by its pristine setting and rich heritage, which includes more than a story or two of the unexplainable nature, including a ghost bride, a bellman who couldn't embrace the concept of retirement, even after his death, and a room that no longer exists.

The bellman seen roaming the hallways, and even assisting guests long after his death, was in this life Sam McAuley, and there's ample documentation to support the story of his existence. The ghost bride is a bit of an iffy tale and morphs with each telling. That said, it's not inconceivable that a poor young lady met with an untimely death on her wedding day some time during the hotel's 126-year history.

The story surrounding room 873 is a little less tangible, but somehow even more gripping than the previous two. According to several accounts, room 873 no longer exists because of a horrific multiple murder that took place in that room, killing an entire family, children and all. It's been said that following the murder, hotel patrons staying in room 873 would notice bloody, child-sized fingerprints appearing randomly on the walls and mirrors. It was creepy, to say the least. These appearances coupled with eyewitness accounts of various ghostly apparitions allegedly belonging to the deceased family members didn't bode well for business. Eventually management decided to board up the room so that patrons couldn't complain about paying good money to share their accommodations with a ghost.

Or at least that's how the story goes.

However, one would think that the local media would have reported a multiple murder, like the one attributed to room 873. No such story has been discovered. Yet the story of room 873 continues in the oral tradition of ghostly legends occurring in the mountains surrounding Banff. And to make the story even more mysterious, many sources have supported the claim that there is indeed a boarded up room at the hotel. That theory is supported, some claim, by a strange spacing between rooms in the hall where the room would have been located. Almost makes you want to book a night just to see if you can find it!

Missing a Foot, Anyone?
At last count, 14 severed feet have washed up along the Pacific coastline. The first such foot story hit the British Columbia

media on August 20, 2007, after a young Washington girl visiting Jedediah Island came across a discarded shoe. When she opened the sock she discovered the severed foot. It was later discovered to have belonged to a man, leaving a curious public to wonder what had become of the person who was once attached to that foot.

The discovery of one severed foot is sad, and certainly disconcerting; the discovery of a second foot just six days later sent alarm bells ringing, especially since the owner of the first foot had yet to be identified. Was it possible that the two feet came from two individuals who had been murdered? If so, why? Were they connected to the illegal drug industry? Or was there some other motive that contributed to their demise.

Between the first discovery and the writing of this book, 10 feet have been discovered along the coast of BC and another four along Washington's shoreline. Investigators have determined that in some of these cases the feet had become disarticulated from the body because of natural decay and that they had sunk because of their shoes' heavy rubber soles.

In some cases DNA testing confirmed the feet belonged to individuals who had gone missing and were thought to have died of natural causes or committed suicide. In one case a foot inside a hiking boot, discovered at Sasamat Lake on November 4, 2011, was identified as belonging to a fisherman who went missing in 1987. But not every DNA test yielded a result, leaving residents to wonder if at least some of these finds were the result of homicide. It's hard to imagine that a human leg bone and foot discovered in a black plastic bag, like the one that washed ashore in Seattle, were a result of anything other than a homicide.

Statistics point to foul play as well. In 2008, after the third foot had surfaced, Simon Fraser University entomologist Gail Anderson told the *Vancouver Province* that although it's not uncommon for extremities to detach from a body as it decomposes, it's extremely rare for them to float. The discovery of three feet in such a short time frame was referred to as "curious." There's no mention of what experts suggest finding 10 in just a few short years might represent, other than another one of Canada's most baffling mysteries.

Summer Tragedy

Canoe Lake, in Algonquin Park, Ontario, is a summertime oasis for outdoor enthusiasts. The area has a magical quality to it—the kind of allure that has drawn researchers from various scientific disciplines interested in studying the area's biodiversity with the same intensity as it has drawn writers and artists, such as Tom Thomson. Thomson's creative juices flowed best amid the tall pines and rippled waters of Algonquin Park. He knew the area intimately, having worked there as a fire ranger and fishing guide, and so on July 8, 1917, Thomson packed his gear and readied his canoe, as he had many times before, for a solitary fishing trip on Canoe Lake.

Thomson never returned from that fishing trip. And despite several eyewitness accounts pinpointing the artist's location throughout the day, exactly what happened to the man has never been determined, making his one of this country's most prevailing mysteries.

Thompson's canoe was located the same day he set off for his fated trip; his body wasn't discovered until eight days later. Although there was a four-inch bruise on his temple, Thomson's death was ruled an accidental drowning.

However, not everyone was comfortable with that declaration. Thomson's body seemed to have been hastily buried in a local cemetery before any of his family members could arrive at the location. Some officials thought Thomson's head injury was too specific to have been caused by a fall, pointing to the possibility that the artist had been in some kind of altercation prior to his death.

There've been many theories about what might have happened to the adventurist painter. One suggests that Thomson's fiancé had a jilted lover who wasn't ready to give up on his girl and confronted Thomson. Another theory posits that Thomson stumbled across a draft dodger who killed him so that he could not reveal the dodger's location. Yet another bizarre idea revolved around the belief that a strange weather phenomenon whipped up tornado-like winds that capsized Thomson's canoe.

Almost a century later and the mystery is as captivating now as it was when it happened. And if you have the inclination, you can do your own sleuthing on the case by logging on to www.canadianmysteries.ca and check out the file entitled "Death On A Painted Lake: The Tom Thomson Tragedy."

ABOUT THE ILLUSTRATORS

Roger Garcia

Roger Garcia is a self-taught freelance illustrator based in Edmonton who works in acrylics, ink and digital media. His illustrations have been published in humour books, children's books, newspapers and educational material.

When Roger is not at home drawing, he can be seen facilitating cartooning workshops at various elementary schools, camps and local art events. Roger also enjoys participating with colleagues in art shows, painting murals in schools and public places.

Peter Tyler

Peter is a graduate of the Vancouver Film School Visual Art and Design, and Classical animation programs. Though his ultimate passion is in filmmaking, he is also intent on developing his draftsmanship and storytelling, with the aim of using those skills in future filmic misadventures.

Graham Johnson

Graham Johnson is an Edmonton-based illustrator and graphic designer. When he isn't drawing or designing, he…well…he's always drawing or designing! On the off-chance that you catch him not doing one of those things, he's probably cooking, playing tennis or poring over other illustrations.

Patrick Hénaff

Born in France, Patrick Hénaff is mostly self-taught and is a versatile artist who has explored a variety of mediums under many different influences. He now uses primarily pen and ink to draw and then processes the images on computer. He is particularly interested in the narrative power of pictures and tries to use them as a way to tell stories, whether he is working on comic pages, posters, illustrations, cartoons or concept art.

Roly Wood

Roly grew up in Indian River, Ontario. He has worked in Toronto as a freelance illustrator, and was also employed in the graphic design department of a landscape architecture firm specializing in themed retail and entertainment design.

In 2004 he wrote and illustrated a historical comic book set in Lang Pioneer Village near Peterborough, Ontario.

Roly currently lives and works as a freelance illustrator in Calgary, Alberta with his wife, Kerri, and their dog, Hank.

Djordje Todorovic

Djordje Todorovic is an artist/illustrator living in Toronto, Ontario. He first moved to the city to go to York University to study fine arts. It was there that he got a taste for illustrating while working as the illustrator for his college paper, *Mondo Magazine.* He has since worked on various projects and continues to perfect his craft. Aside from his artistic work, Djordje devotes his time volunteering at the Print and Drawing Centre at the Art Gallery of Ontario. When he is not doing that, he is out trotting the globe. He has illustrated three other books.

ABOUT THE AUTHOR

Lisa Wojna

Bestselling author Lisa Wojna has authored or co-authored more than 20 books for Blue Bike Books, including the bestselling titles *Weird Canadian Laws* and the *Bathroom Book of Canadian Quotes*. She has also written many other non-fiction books. Having worked in the community newspaper industry as a writer and journalist, she has travelled all over Canada from the windy prairies of Manitoba to northern British Columbia and even to the wilds of Africa. Although writing and photography have been a central part of her life for as long as she can remember, it's the people behind every story that are her motivation and give her the most fulfillment.